# SOUL CALL

## When was the last time you listened to your SELF?

# SOUL CALL

**When was the last time you listened to your SELF?**

*Abhay*

Notion Press

5 Muthu Kalathy Street, Triplicane,

Chennai - 600 005

First Published by Notion Press 2014



ISBN: 978-93-84391-92-8

# Dedication

My tribute to the men & women who were born before their times

...my tribute to those who were destined not to be understood

...my tribute to those who lived to love and loved to live

...my tribute to those who made a difference to whatever they touched

...my tribute to those who were born to give but were destined to be deprived

...my tribute to the man I always wanted to discover in myself

# Prologue

*"The unexamined life is not worth living"* – *Socrates*

In our rush for success, life just seems to go on, in a meaningless manner. And one day, somewhere at the end of the summer or in the autumn of life, it appears that we were not there to live it. We just were not there, to savour the moments. We did not listen to what life had been whispering to us.... what our soul had to tell us. We were too busy to be truly there in 'that' moment of life. We were too busy worrying about what could be, what we were missing and where we wanted to reach. We had been too busy fantasizing about the destination and missed the whole beautiful journey, little knowing that each moment of the journey was a destination, complete by itself, full of meaning and purpose, full of beauty and grandeur.

And in those unending years of our sleep – life simply passes by.

> Those beautiful moments, which could have easily been lived, just disappear in the haze of time.
>
> Those loving touches we never felt, remain only as part of our sub conscious.
>
> Those feelings which make life worth living, get lost in the folds of time.
>
> Those souls who have been there with us for so many lifetimes come and go away un-recognized – always a smile away, a touch away but we are too enmeshed in the role we are playing.

But then, sometimes if you are lucky enough, comes that mysterious phase in life when the past seems to fall in place, the present becomes meaningful and the future seems to acquire a purpose. And then you realize that perhaps this is the true beginning… that it is spring, really and truly, only when you awaken….it is morning only when you come out of your stupor.

It is then and only then that we truly start living … living with awareness … living with a purpose and most importantly start savouring life.

This book is about reliving those lost moments, discovering the meaning & significance of those ordinary yet profound moments of life. It is about beginning afresh with a new awareness… with a renewed sense of identification with our true

SELF….. it is about realizing what really matters in Life.

I was indeed fortunate to recapture what my Soul had been calling out to me….. I sincerely hope this book would prove to be a catalyst in putting you in touch with yours

*Kuch aur bhi hain meri zindagi ki tasweerein*
*main woh nahin jo yaron ne mujhe samjha hai*

*Unknown*

*[There are many more dimensions to my life; I am much more than what my buddies have known about me]*

# Contents

# Contents of this Chronicle

This chronicle has not been divided into any sections nor is it arranged in any form of order – for life does not follow any order… also because this book is not about logic or formulas or techniques & tools for success.

All the writings in this book are outpourings of the heart and the mind. All the thoughts shared herein are deeply held as well as firmly believed. These thoughts are also a revelation. They are a revelation because, although they were always there deep down within me, they were uncovered suddenly and I was face to face with them. It was like seeing your own face for the first time.

I have simply shared the values, beliefs and experiences of my life which may provide you with an insight – an insight which may enable you to lead a better and more enriching life

However, what follows can be said to contain four categories of experiences or thoughts in a completely random manner

## Ripples in Time

These are incidents which appeared so very insignificant and yet had such deep meaningful impact on my mind. How the meaning and significance of these events had impacted my life was realized by me much later. These incidents, I understand today, shaped a lot of my thought process as I went along and had a deep impact on my persona.

Those moments in a way revealed the pathway that life has taken me along.

## Souls from the Mist

Our near and dear ones as well as the people that we are destined to interact with....they are the ones who make this life worth living. Whether it is the friends we have chosen or the people we are thrown in contact with – we share a deep and abiding connection with them. These connections are far more than just chance happenings. These people have come into our lives, because they had something significant to contribute in our life ....and we in theirs'.

These souls deserve our gratitude. We may never see it very clearly but the fact remains that our lives would not have been the same without the veiled presence of these souls. We have met them for a definite purpose, a purpose only time will reveal.

Such narratives are a tribute to the souls that I have shared some time on this earth with. The souls who came in touch to impart some of the most valuable lessons in life..... the souls which taught me the meaning of beauty, happiness, contentment, honesty, fairness, compassion and above all LOVE.

## Hearts on Fire

What is life without emotions? The only memories that stay with us are of the incidents which have been emotionally seared into our brains. It is our feelings which make us human. It is our heart that drives us. Whatever we feel deeply about ultimately becomes the driving force of our lives. My life would be worth nothing if my mind was full of knowledge and my heart empty.

This is where I share the outpourings of my heart. The thoughts, feelings & desire that clawed at my heart have found expression here. Whatever the heart yearns for stays with you forever. These feelings & longings are what make me vulnerable and because they make me vulnerable, they make me alive.

I have shared the moments which make me human. I share the emotions which made this life worth living.

## Earthy Values

If a man is to be at peace he has to live by his values, ideas & convictions.... which he holds and which became deep rooted through experiences. The values & convictions shared here are the ones which life chose to teach me and which I chose to hold on to.

As far as I am concerned, these convictions have not only stood the test of time, they have also stood the test of heart and that tiny voice inside which goes by the name of conscience. While no conviction can be all encompassing, it is the essence or the principle involved which remains the beacon. It is that crux which should always prevail while the form and detail may undergo any change.

I hope these values will keep me rooted as long as I live and thereafter... rooted to all that is worth holding on to... all that makes us evolved creatures... all that makes us human beings... all that is relevant for being human.

### So how should you read this chronicle?

The book can be read from any point to any other point and would not require a sequential reading. Each passage is complete on its own and yet these passages are like pearls in a necklace... the beauty of which can be perceived only when they are seen as a whole. The entire book would provide an enriching experience which would be more than the sum of its parts.

It is not meant to be read in a rush. It must be savoured, digested and deeply felt. While it can be read at random from anywhere, I would advise you to read it sequentially at leisure and try and contemplate on what has been shared. I am sure you would be able to identify with the narrative in this chronicle in a lot of places and link it with some happening, feeling, relationship or conviction from your own life.

Read, relish, contemplate ... and listen carefully to what your own Self has been trying to tell you.... and if this chronicle can help you to connect with your Self and create a better life for yourself and your loved ones, it would have been worth writing it.

The purpose of this book is not to provide information... it is to help in your transformation...

*Harry Potter to Dumbledore in his death-dream "Is it real or is it happening inside my head?" Dumbledore "Of course it is happening inside your head Harry, but why should that mean that it is not real?"*

**- Harry Potter & the Deathly Hallows (by JK Rowlings)**

*"May you live all the days of your life"*
*- Jonathan Swift*

# El Dorado

For years, on my way to the office I passed this house. A ramshackle building it was, with almost no footpath in the front – unpainted walls and doors and windows. And yet what caught my attention was the brand new name plate attached next to the entrance, which in very neat letters said 'El Dorado'. It somehow told me that in this house lived a man with a dream - a man who dreamed of far off lands or perhaps achievements. That small plate was a sign of hope. It was also a sign of the will to dream, a sign that aspirations exist in every nook and corner of the world. Where ever there is a human heart beating there is also a longing perhaps – a longing to become something - to have a home of your dreams.

Years passed and I saw no change in the appearance of the house. It remained as ramshackle, as ever. In fact it got worse. And then one day I saw the plate was broken. Both the ends hung separately, screwed to the wall. One had the 'El' and the other 'Dorado'. The dream was broken. Days passed and I always made it a point to look. But the plate hung in the same position, un-cared for and un-repaired. And then I knew that the man who put it up years ago was dead. No, I did not see his dead body… nor had I seen him alive for that matter. But it did not matter, whether he was actually alive or dead. A dream had died. And with the death of a dream, some part of the human spirit also dies.

I knew that a spirit had died. What good is a body after that!

I just hope someone puts up a sign very soon. The dream of an 'El Dorado' is too important to lose. It really is painful when the human spirit gives up. That is the only real death.

But it did not matter, whether he was actually alive or dead. A dream had died. And with the death of a dream, some part of the human spirit also dies.

*"The true measure of a man is how he treats someone who can do him absolutely no good."*
*– Samuel Johnson*

# Seven Rupees to Nirvana

I had just got admitted to college and that morning which was not different from any other morning I was going to attend work as an Articled Clerk. Half way to the bus stop and close to the railway station this boy came up to me. More or less my age, obviously well built like me but what struck me was his open and honest face. He approached me frankly and asked for help. He had dropped his money somewhere and was not in a position to buy his return ticket back to a suburban town. Like me in those days he was a martial arts enthusiast - in short he identified with me and wanted my help to get back home. How much, would he need, I asked. "Seven Rupees!" he said. I cringed for all I had were two rupees, just enough to get me to office and back. It also happened to be the end of the month so I knew there was no money at home either. I looked at his face again. I could rely on him I decided. I resolved to help him. My first stop was my cousin's house although I was not very hopeful about getting much help. It did prove to be futile. I took him home, rummaged through the house and somehow managed to scrape up seven rupees, which I handed over to him not knowing whether I would ever see him again.

I never did see him again.

But he was yet to contribute something into my life without my coming face to face with him.

Almost a month went by. One day when I came back from office my mother told me that some boy I had helped by way of giving him his train fare had come to see me. Since she did not know him he stood outside and talked to her for quite sometime, appreciated the fact that she did not trust a complete stranger. By the end of that half an hour she was even willing to let him in but he left.

He had not returned the seven rupees. But he gave me something far more precious. He gave me the ability to trust and have faith in humanity. His coming back told me that it is worthwhile to help people even though some of them may not acknowledge or deserve it.

His coming back ensured that I would not give up my giving nature which was so essentially me. It was the best investment of my life. It came good. It has lasted all my life. I keep drawing from it every time I make a bad investment.

Those seven bucks ensured that I would remain myself for the rest of my life. If that isn't *nirvana* what is?

> He gave me the ability to trust and have faith in humanity. His coming back told me that it is worthwhile to help people even though some of them may not acknowledge or deserve it.

*"A promise made is a debt unpaid."*
*– Robert W. Service*

# Loose Ends of Life

"If ever I get married, you come and shoot me." He wrote this note and gave it to me. I gave him an identical note written by me. We were all of 10 years old then and dead serious about our vow. The notes were kept away in safe places for they might be needed some day.

I danced at his wedding.

A… was the first friend I made in my life. He became my first friend in a city where I spent the first year totally traumatized in a predominantly girls' school. I hated everything about Calcutta back then. Most of all I hated the school I went to. Lonely and isolated, I could not make friends in the school where I was ridiculed by the teachers and shunned by my classmates. But I could not really blame them because I went around spitting at each and everything. There were times when I wet my pants in the classroom itself. I had not been able to handle the trauma of leaving my cousins and relatives and coming to a far off city to spend the rest of my life. We had come to Calcutta forever. And forever was a long period for me at that age.

I complained about the teachers. I refused to drink water in that school and refused to use the toilets as well. I did everything possible, so that I would be taken out of the school. And it got me nothing but trouble. The hellish year somehow passed and then I found A.... The two girl haters were united in their shyness.

There was so much we found in common. And there was much we had to give each other. He introduced me to my first love – BOOKS. We would spend hours in the same room just reading. From Enid Blyton to TinTin, it was a journey through a different world. Perhaps in some way we built up each other's value system. Although he was junior to me by one year in school, physically, he was more than a match for even my seniors. With him around no one dared bully me.

We became inseparable. There was not a single day that we did not spend time with each other. And it was not only us, our families came very close. We would go out for dinners together. Being Punjabis they would have non-vegetarian food and we would stick to the vegetarian stuff. There was complete acceptance of each others' ways of life.

Not once, did we try to influence our eating habits. Right across me A... would have "Tandoori chicken" when I stuck to my "Chana Masala". That is why I never developed any kind of revulsion for non-vegetarian stuff. In fact that is how I learnt to accept ways of life which could be so different from mine.

Some of the very special moments were those Sunday-morning cartoon shows. The Lion of the MGM films has become very much a part of my childhood. My first trip, to a hill station was also with his family. It was thanks only to them that we could manage to go to Shimla.

We fuelled each other's patriotism. We ridiculed together the prevalent communism. We became a formidable team, no matter whether it was a game or a fight. When he bought a pet dog, I took pride in the ownership as well. Those outings, the wonderful times spent together became an integral part of me. There were so many 'firsts' in the times we spent together. That is why perhaps each and every thing is so special.

But then our togetherness was also not meant to last for very long. His father was transferred to Ludhiana in Punjab. We parted after five years. But we did not give up. We wrote regularly and managed a visit now and then. He had grown up to be a robust young man... but still remained, shy as ever. I loved my visits to Ludhiana. The carefree times, the bike rides and the non stop snacking – life had never been so good. Combine it with the thrill of being in Punjab during turbulent times and you would know what a time I had there. I can still remember the feel of the .22 revolver in my hand – I had never expected it to be so heavy. A... gifted me a spent bullet of the same caliber. How he managed that only he knew. I have always carried it with me as a good luck charm.

I remember how much I enjoyed being there for his wedding, which took place at the height of Punjab militancy. I regaled his friends with my jokes and songs. I still remember his young wife laughing unabashedly as I mimicked the drunk 'Baratis' the next day.

He could not make it to my marriage. Slowly our letters became a little less frequent when he took up a job in Bombay. We did meet twice during his visits to Calcutta. Preeti, my wife, also liked the young man who in so many ways was still a boy. That shy smile was still the same.

And then one evening in 1989 when I came back from office, Preeti quietly handed over a letter to me. It was from A...'s elder brother and it informed us that A... had died of Meningitis after a few days of illness.

After years I cried.

I cried for all that was a part of me and had been lost. I cried because I saw his young wife's face. I cried for the young son who had lost his father. I really wanted to go and visit his family. And yet at another level I was afraid of facing them. In any case, the circumstances prevailing then did not allow me to make that visit. And as time rolled by I never could really make that visit. Now and then I would think of going but then some priority or the other took precedence over that visit.

A... is gone. But in so many ways he remains very much what he was – an integral part of what is me. As much as my youth and childhood belong to me, he belongs to my youth and childhood. He can never really go away from a dimension, which I visit now and then. He still lives and breathes in that realm.

But there is something that I have failed to do in this realm, which pinches me. In some way or the other I feel I failed myself. I failed him. I failed his wife. I owed it to all of us to make that trip to Ludhiana. It is a pilgrimage, which is still due. I know this is what I need to forgive myself.

I do not know how I will face them. But face them I have to. I do not even know if they will recognize me. But I do know some part of me will be at peace with myself when I do it.

It is a loose end of my life I need to tie up. I hope life will be kind enough to allow me to do that.

As much as my youth and childhood belong to me, he belongs to my youth and childhood. He can never really go away from a dimension, which I visit now and then. He still lives and breathes in that realm.

*"The greatest enemy of clear language is insincerity." –George Orwell*

# The Fashion of Political Correctness

This is the age of clichés, an age where everyone has a stereotyped opinion. And even more importantly, has a voice. People are well informed – thanks to the media. People are intelligent and logical. People are eager to talk. And when they talk they are heard – again thanks to the media.

And that is also the tragedy of these times. Logic and intelligence have no depth and in these times they hold sway. We have stopped questioning what has been repeated so often. That is why this is the age of clichés. That is why principles like "Justice" & "Liberty" have become a hostage to political postures like "Secularism" & "Socialism".

It is fashionable to cut old beliefs down to size. It is the 'in' thing to mouth all the inane and right sounding ideas on peace & religion. We love parroting the politically correct things as opposed to correct things although they may sound politically incorrect... and in today's context political correctness has been reduced to a euphemism for hypocrisy. The society at large is already paying a heavy price for this hypocrisy. The real issues are being swept under the carpet and one day sure enough they come back to haunt you.

We debate about the proof of existence of Hindu Gods. We debate about ways of implementing the Islamic code. We quarrel about the authority of church. But we never go into the wisdom and philosophy behind the teachings. We do not question the correctness of the teachings. We seem to be either too busy propagating them or debunking them. The secular ones debunk their own religion in order to appear 'holier than thou'. The zealots are busy conveying the sentiments of their community whenever they perceive any affront to what they hold so dear.

The basic spirit of religion – the search for truth is well and truly lost. We are either too busy trying to exercise our right to say "My God is better than yours." or too busy pronouncing the greatness of every religion. Our focus is on looking for forensic proofs whereas these are of no relevance. It does not matter whether Krishna spoke *'Gita'* or not. What matters is whether what Gita says is the truth or not! It does not matter whether Christ could cure with his touch or not. What matters is whether he talked about the right ways or not.

It is the inner core, which must be sought out from these religions. Their historical correctness or social norms which are incidental are not the core issue.

But where is the spirit of questioning; the spirit of trying to understand? Either we are too busy pasting greatness on any and every idea or busy rejecting it in our bid to appear secular. The spirit, which brought great ideas to the human race, seems to be lost, for we are either too busy conforming or too busy rebelling. The common man has a voice today. But it appears that the common man today is either a brainwashed one or a pretentious intellectual. He does not seem to care as to WHAT is correct.

He is too busy trying to be 'politically correct'. The truth, be damned. A little bit of applause is far more important! Isn't it?

The common man has a voice today. But it appears that the common man today is either a brainwashed one or a pretentious intellectual. He does not seem to care as to WHAT is correct.

*"It's always a pleasure to find something that matters."* – *Don Cornelius*

# The Young Boy Lost in the Streets of Karauli

Although he had been born in that small town, he had mixed feelings about the place. He was always awed, by the *Haveli* (*old fashioned private mansion*), he had been born in. It was such an imposing structure made of stone. To him it appeared so timeless and indomitable. He found the open-air toilets quite funny and a source of adventure everyday. The streets were paved with long slabs of stones, they were dusty but not filthy.

But he hated the way his mother and maternal grandmother wailed, at the end of every visit. But this time around, at the age of 7 he was trying to explore the place a little more. The local kids had been friendly and he spent a lot of time playing with them at the gates of the *haveli*.

That day almost a dozen of them gathered and were in a boisterous mood. Soon a race was on, which he also joined. The bunch took off in that narrow winding lane which went uphill slightly, took a dip and then wound down. But the other kids were older and he was no match for their speed or stamina. By the time they reached the slope, he had been outrun and the area seemed, totally unfamiliar to him. He stopped there and stood panting. Within seconds, the others were out of sight. Suddenly, he was scared… he was lost. But oh God, he recognized the cottage he stood in front of. It belonged to that old witch. Now, he was really scared! Despite himself, he started sobbing. He had been told all about the witch and how she hated small kids. The local kids always ran past her place hurling abuses at her.

To his horror, that was the moment the old hag chose to come out of her hut. His attention was riveted to the white hair and that ugly wrinkled face. She mumbled something to him, which he could not follow. He was not totally familiar with the dialect and the manner in which the people spoke there. The Witch took him by his hand and led him inside. Petrified, he simply followed. She made him sit and came back with a glass of water. So she was not going to harm him after all.

He drank the water and that is when he noticed the eyes. They seemed so sad. He knew then that she was harmless.

By this time a few others had gathered and enquiries had started. 'Are you Sunto's son' they asked him. He declined. His mother's name was Shanti. That's it; he was Sunto's son they concluded. He was led away to the *haveli*. It was then, he realised that all along he had been hardly 100 metres from the *haveli* in the same lane. He went back but the incident made a deep impression on him. That face and those eyes stayed with him.

I still cannot forget those sad eyes. I think I know why they were so sad. I have learnt not to judge people just by their looks. I try and see beyond the skin-deep appearance. I also understand that when a lot of people judge you just by your looks, you get sad eyes like that.

That boy is no longer lost. He has found himself. He is not going to give anyone sad eyes. That is my promise to that boy.

The Witch took him by his hand and led him inside. Petrified, he simply followed. She made him sit and came back with a glass of water. So she was not going to harm him after all.

*"Light enters through a wound....".*

# Pain – The Hidden Friend

I was very calm. And that, in itself was quite strange. It was the final competition of the National Convention of Miltonians. The venue was Bombay and the year 1996. I sat in the competitors' row awaiting my turn to perform impromptu Dramatics. The day had been spent in intense pain. My mouth was full of ulcers and it had been growing worse every day. It was the fourth day since our arrival and with each passing day the pain had been increasing. So much so that, that day I could not eat anything. Even the attempt to have a spoonful of curd rice had left me writhing in pain. Five minutes before the competition I coated my mouth with an analgesic ointment. And amidst the thunderous cheering of over 450 audience, I took my seat along side 19 other competitors.

When my turn came I went up and performed in a way that came naturally to me. By the time I finished I knew it was one of the best performances.

And as I jumped off the stage, A...... told me that I had "Done it." Nevertheless I could not be sure. We would win the shield if I managed to win this competition. In so many ways there was a sense of déjà vu.

I had won as the announcement during the awards nite informed me. With that announcement it also became clear that Calcutta Chapter had won the shield. And as I received the last cup to be given away, I choked. AT LAST I HAD LAID A GHOST TO REST.

For six years I had lived with a raw wound – a wound, which had gone in deep. I had received that wound in a very similar situation that had just taken place. The year was 1990 and the venue Bangalore. I was leading the Calcutta chapter then. Both Calcutta and the host chapter were tied at 4 cups each. A tie - breaker was applied and the shield was to be decided by a Dramatics competition. The onus fell on me to represent Calcutta. Shashi from Bangalore went up first and did a very competent job. Then I went up and as I read the slip, which gave me the topic a tremendous roar went up from the crowd – I was to enact the MILT Trainer & Director taking a MILT class. I was already acknowledged as one of the best mimics by Miltonians all over the country and one of my spoofs of the Director was immensely popular. But perhaps it was my attempt to be a little different that did me in. Somewhere during that performance I faltered slightly. In that moment I lost.

I lost by one single point. I also lost the shield for my Chapter. It felt as if a spear had gone through my heart. There were tremendous celebrations all around as the host chapter Miltonians went crazy. And amongst all this I was holding back my tears with great effort. I could not face my team for I had let them down. But they were all with me. Somewhere deep down, that defeat changed me. I never really could take out that spear. That wound remained raw for all those six years. When I competed in Bombay it was not just the physical pain I was fighting. It was this raw pain, which never really went away that I was struggling with.

This win, six years later in Bombay finally enabled me to lay the ghost to rest. And again I choked during my acceptance speech. I had proved something to myself. And that is why this victory was not ordinary. I had not competed with anyone else. I did not really beat the best 19 from the rest of the country. I beat myself to the best performance I had made.

As I look back, I can say that it was the wound I received in 1990, that really made me strive for excellence and give off my best. The pain I carried all these years is what really gave me the drive to win.

So many times in life pain comes and stays with us. And how we hate it.... little realizing that pain too is a friend – a friend, which enables us to come out with our best, a friend which makes us fight.

Sometimes it comes as an ache, which gets rejuvenated with every breath, sometimes it comes like the blow of a sledge hammer and sometimes like a knife in the heart. Whether, it is the pain of a defeat, or the pain of a broken relationship, or the ache of an unfulfilled one, it does make us deeply aware of our core. It creates a vacuum within the deepest recesses of our hearts and psyche, which we desperately try to fill.

But the paradox is that whenever we accept it and make it an inseparable part of ourselves it makes us grow. It makes us reach deep within to perform without. We can never remain at the level when we received our share of pain. It is only then perhaps that we make an extraordinary effort to live up to our potential.

On the other hand, when we try and block this gift of pain or find external solutions to ease it, we end up at the other end of the spiral. That is when we actually start running away from ourselves. That is when we start losing. I can never lose because of the presence of pain; I can only lose because of the absence of 'me'.

Whether the pain is physical or mental it always gives us an edge. Unless we grind our teeth that extra effort does not seem to come by. Perhaps that is why sportsman who fall ill or get injured during a match, come out with superlative effort. Even on the physical level the mechanism of pain protects us. Just imagine what would happen if you did not jerk your hand away when you touched something hot.

I can recollect various instances in my own life when pain made me become more of what I was capable of becoming:-

- I faced the ignominy of going blank in a fantasizing competition. That humiliation enabled me to excel on that forum.
- I started my first year of graduation by getting zero in Accounts. That jolt made me a Chartered Accountant.
- I messed up a recitation on school stage. It stayed with me, and that is what made me work towards gaining confidence so that I could go up to the stage in any gathering.
- Talking to a girl was a very painful exercise and brought many an embarrassing moments in my youth. That is what gave me the grit to develop into a person who would not flinch from talking to anyone
- My lack of ability to express myself clearly and confidently was a deterrent to my professional growth and brought me humiliation a couple of times. That gave me the determination to work towards becoming a competent professional.
- When it came to money and forthrightness on the work front I was too diffident. I lost

> heavily because of this. Never got the salary I deserved, for I could not ask for it. The pain this inability gave built up over the years and finally gave me the ability and fire to be not only forthright but a tough professional as well.

How I worked at it is a different thing. But the point is what made me do it? It was the pain, which drove me every time. I suppose I responded correctly and that is why pain proved to be a friend.

None of us really like it, but in its wake pain does bring to surface our inherent qualities. Maybe in some ways it tells us that to fill the vacuum inside, we must dig deeper within and respond in the best way we can. And when we do that we can see pain for what it is – a true friend; a friend, who shows us that you don't ever really win if you have never lost.

Perhaps the most important lessons in life stay with us in the form of pain! Why should I want to get rid of them? Pain is as much mine as any happiness is. Perhaps it is a better friend for it never really deserts us and makes every happiness that much sweeter. Not that, we need to court pain. It does tend to come when we deserve it the most. The only problem is we are not wise enough to see its role in our lives when it strikes us.

At times pain brings us in touch with who we essentially are.

It makes us confront ourselves.

It shakes us up and wakes us up.

It stirs our insides and makes us question our deepest motives. Most importantly it raises the level of our awareness. When we are in pain we see the world more clearly. We respond from our deepest core. That is when we truly and sincerely respond to life.

Behind most achievements and creativity – pain lurks in some form or the other. Most poets could touch our heart-strings only when they had experienced pain. The life forms on our planet emerge in a painful process. All conscious beings give birth in pain. The greatest of achievers in history went through tremendous personal pain, which propelled them into determined activity. Whether it is hurt, pride or emotional trauma, it is this unknown quality of pain, which has always pushed a human being up to a level where he ends up achieving something, which he himself never thought he was capable of. In one way or the other creation and achievement is linked to pain.

There is a man worshipped by millions all over the world, whose teachings have guided the lives of many generations. His mission in life was deeply propelled by pain. To begin with he was a man who had never seen or felt pain. He never experienced unhappiness during the initial phase of his life. He had not seen disease or ill health. All the happiness and the comforts in the world had nurtured Prince Siddhartha. With all this he remained an ordinary Prince.

It was pain that made him Gautam Buddha.

Most importantly it raises the level of our awareness. When we are in pain we see the world more clearly. We respond from our deepest core. That is when we truly and sincerely respond to life.

*"Plant a tree, whose shade we know we may never sit under...." –Old saying*

# The Old Man and The Tree

It is a huge tree now, the biggest in the locality. One of the biggest that I have seen, spread across two buildings and taller than both of them.

I saw it being born.

He was old, frail and bent – an old man we thought was cranky, who would berate us for being loud. As we, a bunch of school kids, played the improvised form of cricket which we called 'Hand cricket', I would see him, carry his watering can to water the sapling he had planted on the footpath of the empty plot. By the time I was in college, it had still not developed a very significant presence. And then I forgot all about it.

And one insignificant day as I walked down the lane, the sheer size of the tree struck me as awesome. And in a moment its beginning flashed before my eyes. I could literally 'see' the old man bent over the sapling – nurturing it with dedication day after day.

The old man has now been dead for more than three decades. The empty plot which was 'developed' now has a huge building on it. But the sapling which the old man had planted has outgrown and continues to overshadow what people could build. The seeds we leave behind not only outlast us, they outlast generations. They continue to contribute long after we may have gone.

Have I planted something which will outlast me?

The seeds we leave behind not only outlast us, they outlast generations. They continue to contribute long after we may have gone.

*"Fairy tales are more than true; not because they tell us that dragons exist, but because they tell us that dragons can be beaten." – G.K. Chesterton*

# Call of the Primal

It was a primal sound. They were singing, yet those primitive sounds could only be described guttural. The movements were some sort of a dance. The dimly lit courtyard and the rattle of the chains which they wore all over them made it all the more eerie. And yet it was a thanksgiving dance.

In that remote small town of Rajasthan it was a quiet summer night. I had been invited for this thanksgiving ritual to our 'Panditji's' (priest) house. A month ago a snake had bitten his wife. She had been cured because he invoked "Gogaji", neither a hospital…nor doctors; she owed her life to this supernatural intervention.

The ritual being performed was the gratitude expressed to "Gogaji". In that remote region where snake bites were common and hospitals rare and far off, it was 'Gogaji' who proved to be the saviour of the victims. His small temples dotted the landscape here and there. Superstition?? Well, there are hundreds who claim to have survived the poisonous bites only through the rituals performed at these small temples for 'snake bites'!!

Miraculous or not, I did watch a ritual which had survived hundreds of years. There is so much hidden in the remote areas of Rajasthan (India) which is unfathomable. This is a place where you manage both – to touch history and experience it as well.

There is so much hidden in the remote areas of Rajasthan (India) which is unfathomable. This is a place where you manage both – to touch history and experience it as well.

*"I long to accomplish a great and noble task, but it is my chief duty to accomplish small tasks as if they were great and noble."*
*– Helen Keller*

# Liftman – a Lesson in Excellence

It was an old building and so was the elevator that bore the load of hundreds of people who frequented that building. I worked on the 4th floor of that building for almost a year and so was obliged to use the lift almost every day.

The frontage of this lift was quite broad and its grilled gates had to be shut manually, as a result liftmen had been assigned to do this duty on shift basis. The liftman would be seated on a stool and would stretch out to open and shut the twin grilled gates at each floor. It was a cumbersome and thankless job and you could see the listless way in which these liftmen performed this task hour after hour, day in and day out. Most of the time when the gates were pushed in order to close them, they would bounce back because they had been pushed too hard or it would take a couple of shoves before they clicked shut and the lift could move.

But there was someone who turned this mundane act into an art. With two neat flicks of his wrist he would send the gates smoothly into their sockets. The gates would click shut neatly every time.

It was a treat to watch this liftman do his job. He taught me that you could bring excellence to every job you are assigned. Being excellent is also an attitude. You need not be a scientist or a painter in order to be excellent.

There is so much talk about excellence nowadays. With more and more sophisticated products coming on to the shelves, with latest technology enabling sleeker and high performing gadgets, excellence has somehow become synonymous with glitz. And yet we rarely notice small instances of excellent skill or service. We manage to ignore or dismiss people performing those small acts of excellence which make life so beautiful.

The world today needs more such liftmen who can teach us the meaning of excellence. The Management Institutes would do well to honour such instances of excellence and not allow this word to become mere jargon devoid of any connection with real day to day life.

For excellence is all around us, just beneath the surface. We fail to register this excellence, maybe because we simply take it for granted. Excellence is there in the delight that you take in the perfect cup of tea that your vendor serves you every time; it sits there on the desk in the shape of flowers which your secretary arranges every day on your desk in an ever new beautiful manner; it is there in the relief which you feel every time your physio gets you back on your feet and it is reflected in the admiration you feel for the way in which your wife can whip up amazing dishes at every party in your house.

There are so many moments in a day when excellence sits beside us… only if we care to notice.

Sometimes it takes a simple liftman to wake you up to this simple truth.

He taught me that you could bring excellence to every job you are assigned. Being excellent is also an attitude. You need not be a scientist or a painter in order to be excellent.

*The more we live guided from within,*
*the greater our control over outer events*
*in the great game of life.*
*For when we live at our own center,*
*in super consciousness,*
*we live in the only true freedom there is.*
*– Omar Khayyam's Rubaiyat*

# Staying Ahead of The Competition

The people in this age seem to be very aware and well informed. Books on self- improvement techniques flood the market. Various courses offer short cuts to a new improved you. "Attitude" seems to be the buzz - word. Everyone seems to know how important positive attitude is. Time management techniques, public speaking & grooming courses are available next door. Everyone argues that people today are far more aware and well informed than they ever were.

Perhaps, in this age we are well informed, but are we more aware? Are we talking about the same things that the wise ones talked about? Everyone seems to be talking about self-improvement, growth, attitude & positive thinking but the question is how many of us truly understand the spirit of these words. Aren't we just skimming the surface?

For instance, hasn't the phrase 'positive thought process' come to mean – 'go and get success at any cost.' Was this meant to convey a win at any cost syndrome? Even children today are being taught aggression as a technique to make them succeed. We seem to be telling the young that you must learn the latest technique to defeat others so that you may win in the game of life. But then, just USING the techniques to stay ahead can only create conflicts within.

Haven't we got it all wrong! Never ever have the 'positive attitude' and the 'spirit of winning' been so badly misinterpreted than in these times. We have got it all the other way round. We are teaching the young to just put on the symptoms that generally come with success. We are not teaching them that success comes only as a result of achievement.

No wonder that the most beautiful forms of healing and meditation have been reduced to fads and fashion. Lack of in depth grasp and superficial understanding of such things has belittled a lot of traditional disciplines. Seeing this trend one can understand why these disciplines and arts were taught only to a select few in the earlier days. Perhaps the ancients were right, in guarding their knowledge, for when we get something without being entitled to it, we do not really value it, nor do we handle it properly.

We are focused on time management at the cost of life management.

We are focused on personality ethics instead of character ethics.

We are focused on projecting to others what we are not, instead of building on what we are.

We are focused on success rather than achievement.

We are concerned about the standard of living rather than quality of life.

It is precisely because of this wrong focus that there is internal skirmish in most of us. We want our children to succeed in order to make us appear successful. We are not allowing them to flower.

But the fundamentals of life actually are quite simple and one does not need a collection of techniques in the market to be an achiever. These short cuts never work, whereas, if the fundamental principles are in place, we never fail. But the tragedy is that such techniques are being used as substitutes for the real thing. We want success by just learning the tricks of the trade when we should be learning the trade itself.

It is time perhaps to modify the lessons being given to the young. It is time to teach them the difference between information and knowledge and between knowledge and wisdom.

We need to focus at the core and unless we work at the fulcrum - the wheel is bound to wobble. Decorating the hub cannot work. One cannot achieve high speed in life if the fulcrum is not strong & stable and the fact is that the fulcrum of human life is made of time-tested principles like honesty, liberty, justice & compassion. Success in life is merely an outcome of imbibing such principles.

Make your inside clean and your outside will shine.

Take care of your character and your reputation will take care of itself.

Take care of your life and the time will take care of itself.

Get the principles right and the personality will follow.

Get your thoughts right and the ability to speak will follow.

Get your fundamentals right and everything else will take care of itself.

We need to take a small walk inside and the journey to success outside will follow. For until we know the fellow inside all that we learn outside is only HOW to do and not WHAT to do. The frills, style and all the techniques might give you the edge and help ONLY if you focus on your unique gifts and are doing the right things. We can learn all the tricks of public speaking but we can never have a lasting impact on people unless we speak with conviction.

The world has seen far better speakers than M. K. Gandhi. But he was far more effective as a leader because he had character. He was intrinsically a far stronger person and that is why when he told the British "It is time you left" – they left. He worked on the most important parts of himself. It is from lives such as his that we can draw some of the most important lessons. The most crucial lesson to my mind was that power comes from the strength of character and the principles one believes in. It does not come from projecting authority or borrowing someone else's personality.

The persons who make a difference in the lives of the people they touch, no matter which age they live in are persons who are strong at the core – persons who live by principles. They know that their only competition is with their own yesterday. They are secure with their abilities.

Wherever they are, they make a mark by being themselves. They win hearts. They do not beat others. And that is why they stand head and shoulders above others. They do not just work, they express themselves. The young people who are being taught how to elbow ahead of others ought to be taught ways of finding and then following themselves. Let us breed lions and not sheep. For, in the realm of uniqueness, there is no competition!

> The young people who are being taught how to elbow ahead of others ought to be taught ways of finding and then following themselves. Let us breed lions and not sheep. For, in the realm of uniqueness, there is no competition!

*"Keep me away from the wisdom which does not cry, the philosophy which does not laugh and the greatness which does not bow before children."–Kahlil Gibran*

# The Emptiest Pair of Eyes

The 2001 Kargil war was over. Indian armed forces had dealt with the sneak attempt to capture key posts in the Drass and Kargil sector. It was easily one of the bravest counter attacks to rid India of invaders from those heights. So many young officers lost their lives in encounters which were terribly disadvantageous – going up against a well-entrenched enemy shooting down from heights with little cover around. That most jawans, who died were shot in the head and face, was proof of this if at all any was needed.

I had been watching the unfolding events very intently. It was a very emotional charged experience for me. The media brought this war into our drawing rooms. I could feel the reality and the harshness of this war which had been thrust upon us. The officers

& soldiers we saw going out to fight were no longer a statistic or an item in the newspaper. They became real people – with names, families & aspirations – for the rest of the nation, which could only watch. This was a war in which every Indian was involved. For the first time perhaps, the people of this country emotionally connected with the valiant Indian soldiers on such a vast scale. I became obsessed with this war – read every account that was printed. I somehow wanted to reach out to these soldiers. Perhaps that was why such a chance came my way.

I had a plantation project in Rajasthan those days and used to go there frequently. Quite a few of the brave hearts who had lost their lives in the Kargil war were from the Jat Regiment & Rajputana Rifles which hailed from that area. It was some months after the Kargil war that the prominent citizens of the town decided to honour the local martyrs. The bereaved families were to be felicitated at a function. I sat on the dais amongst a dozen prominent citizens & dignitaries. As part of the felicitation ceremony the dignitaries on the dais were also felicitated and presented with shawls. Like others I was also presented with one. The felicitation was followed by speeches. While the speeches went on my eyes were rooted to the enclosure where the families of the soldiers sat. There were wives who had lost their husbands and mothers who had lost their sons. All the speeches in the world sounded meaningless in the face of their loss which I saw writ on their faces. Some of them moved like zombies. Their loss was irreparable and even a fraction of it could not be made up with all the honours that they could be given. One by one these mothers and wives were called up and honoured and felicitated with the cash awards & shawls.

I was writhing in my seat. What had I done, to be felicitated at a function like this one? Truly, I had no business being a 'dignitary' and accepting the shawl that was being conferred upon family members of the soldiers who had made the supreme sacrifice. At the first opportunity, I got up and made my way towards the enclosure where the bereaved family members sat quietly. I knelt beside the mother of a Jat soldier who had laid down his life and gently placed the shawl in her lap as my own small tribute. She looked up…too numb even now to be surprised. Her eyes were blank…the emptiest pair I had ever seen. I could not think anything decent to say. I also did not have the courage to face her for long. So I got up and walked out into the winter sun… but it was a long time before the lump in my throat could dissolve. When such crises come, people like me continue to live in the safety of our homes only because there are some mothers who sent their sons out to die for us. No matter what people do for them in return, it can never be sufficient.

The fact remains that the mother I encountered would have to continue to live with her loss. Nothing would ever be able to fill the emptiness that was a part of her now…an emptiness that would always be reflected in her eyes.

When such crises come, people like me continue to live in the safety of our homes only because there are some mothers who sent their sons out to die for us. No matter what people do for them in return, it can never be sufficient.

*"Love is what you are left with when you let go of all the things you love" – The Buddha*

## Love that You Receive

I do not know whether I deserved it, but the love that I received has formed me into whatever I am. Reading about love being God's energy was fine, but it was only an intellectual exercise. Realizing that it was actually working on you was a revelation. Receiving it was easy, but then the desire to be worthy of it also became important.

So many times in my life, I felt I was perceived to be more than what I was at that point of time and THAT, more than anything else started the process of self improvement Being accepted and loved for what I am, worked like an elixir. Now there is an un-shake-able belief, that I shall always be valued in terms of what I have been, how much I have loved, how much I have contributed in the life of the people around me and not by how much I earned or lost. There is no longer a road to happiness. Happiness is what I ride in this journey of life.

Sometimes, when I try to reminisce about the bygone days all that comes to mind is the time that I spent with loved ones. Why is that? Perhaps because that was the only time that I actually lived.

Once I became conscious of this potent energy, it worked for me in so many ways. Receiving love and giving love has become so much easier. It works all around. All the theories and techniques are useless without it, and once you make love a part of you, everything else starts working. All that really matters in life comes to you. And even more importantly all that does not really matter loses its hold over you.

The smile that I see on the face of a friend; the warmth of the people who work with me; the concern of my parents; the showering of affection of my children; the way my wife clings to me; the way my female friends seek my company and the way my male friends laugh with me or seek advice from me (or pull my leg) – all this, is what, concrete manifestation of LOVE is for me.

This is what makes life worthwhile.

Or would it be more appropriate to say that, this is what MAKES up life – the love that you receive.

Once you make love a part of you, everything else starts working. All that really matters in life comes to you. And even more importantly all that does not really matter loses its hold over you.

*"There is not enough celebration of companionship. Relationships aren't just about eroticism and sexuality."–Francesca Annis*

## Connecting

Connecting with individuals I have a certain affinity with, has brought me so much joy. The labels on relationships have little meaning, for they do not really describe or convey the connection. With different people we connect differently on different planes. The intimacy I share with every individual is quite unique and beautiful. There is no need to define it or label it. The beauty of life can be shared completely only through such connecting. And yet, there is lack of freedom here also. Relationships are always seen through the same colored glasses by most people - aunt, friend's wife, sister's friend, sister-in-law, friend's brother, father-in-law - there has to be a label. But once you are able to break these shackles you truly start connecting. Much is lost if you do not share such intimacy and bonding on a personal basis shorn of any such label, with at least a handful of people.

Connecting with members of the opposite sex, whom I have an affinity with has also been so very important. It has been fulfilling in so many ways - in the way I understand their thoughts, feelings and desires; in the way I interact with them; in the way I understand my own sexuality; in the way that I relate to my own feminine self.

In most societies establishing such a connection is a challenge because they discourage such interactions. Nevertheless, all our relationships can be so very incomplete without such connections.

There is much more to individuals than just being a father, mother, brother, aunt or sister-in-law. Connecting at that subtler level where you can share each other's deepest longings, yearnings and wishes can help you find yourself. The reason why most people are unable to have a healthy relationship with members of the opposite sex is that they are unsure of themselves - scared of their own feelings. The journey to a healthy self-esteem would be incomplete if I am too scared to spend some time with people I like, no matter what their sex is, no matter what the relationship label is.

The labels on relationships have little meaning, for they do not really describe or convey the connection. With different people we connect differently on different planes.

*"When one door of happiness closes, another opens; but often we look so long at the closed door that we do not see the one which has been opened for us."–Helen Keller*

# Lessons from a Life

Some lives make you believe in destiny. Some relationships teach you so much about life. Sometimes you observe a life so closely that you almost see things coming. Sometimes you know what a person really needs or wants in life. Sometimes you live another lifetime through someone else....

I saw and felt his longings so well. It is not that I knew all that he went through. But I did feel and experience his longings and wants. His emotional deposits and need for love was always evident to me. But most of my life I did not have the maturity and wisdom to tackle this knowledge.

When as a teenager, he split with his girl friend I knew something very important to him had been lost by him. Years after his marriage I would tell him that he could discover true happiness whether physical or emotional only through the girl he had lost. Instinctively again, I knew they were destined to meet again – and a fulfillment would take place. It was as if they had to come together to complete something in each other's lives. It did happen and that too in a very deep way. To me, somehow, this union was as natural as snow on the mountain or rain in the forest. And it was destined. What was unusual was that this piece of destiny was so palpably visible.

He did discover the true happiness of a male female relationship. Only it was unfortunate that it had to be after he had ended his marriage – a marriage which again was perhaps destined to end acrimoniously – an end, which was foretold in his horoscope in clear terms a few days after he was born.

I know how "improper" it is to talk about destiny and horoscopes in this day and age. But then life and facts do not follow the scientific establishment or the "rational" mind. Life goes its own way – throwing up things whether palatable, illogical, mysterious or frustrating. Some lives touch you with all of these and give you a ringside view of what it is all about. Some lives bring you understanding about the strange and mysterious ways of destiny. Some lives teach you about the importance of emotion of love in a very concrete manner.

His life has taught me a lot but at his expense, for I understand what really matters in life, without paying for that lesson. I know that taking big decisions is more about who and what we really want in life than about following social compulsions.

For happiness is not a product of society. Society is a spin-off of happy people.

His failings, his weaknesses as well as his strengths – all have been there for me to learn from. His life has been a lesson in reality. His life offers me wisdom if indeed I am entitled to it. Wisdom about what works and what doesn't... how relationships slip when you clutch at them ...how you lose when you want to defeat.... how feeding the ego starves your soul... how people judge you by how you make them feel!!! The emotional needs of a person are not merely needs, they become the mental claws that shape his destiny – decide what he will be – where he will be.

These needs also decide the people who will come into his life, stay in his life and go out of his life.

At times I have felt deeply about what he misses and perhaps what he wants. I cannot help but feel wistful sometimes at what might have been. Then again... who knows all that I wish for him may be there... waiting for him.... at the right time.

The emotional needs of a person are not merely needs, they become the mental claws that shape his destiny – decide what he will be – where he will be.

*"Attitudes are contagious. Are yours worth catching?"*

# The Shadow

He is gone. Whenever I think of him, the only image I get is that of a face full of laughter – eyes which always smiled. That natural and infectious laughter is the most lasting impression of his that I have in my mind. Whenever anyone was in need he always thought of S__ bhai for he was always there for everyone.

But when his end came, no one could do anything for him.

To me he was someone very special. An elder brother cum father figure rolled into one. No matter what kind of help was needed we always thought of him. Not because he had been my father's friend and colleague for the last 30 years, but because of what he was – a man full of compassion and zest for life – a man who was always there, strong immovable & imperturbable.

No one had ever thought that this pillar of strength would be gone so soon. He had been steadily losing weight for some time now. But the mystery was that the disease could not be diagnosed in spite of repeated tests. Not even in the USA with the best of medical technology.

I met him a couple of times in the last few days before his death. I could feel a shadow over him. Although I would not admit to myself, I was scared. I somehow felt that the answer to his problem did not lie in the conventional treatments. It was as if there was a danger from another dimension. A dimension not really understood by us. Of course the symptoms were appearing like a respiratory disease. But I felt it was only the peripheral cause. The real cause lay deeper. It was the presence of a shadow I cannot define or pinpoint.

It was as if I felt the presence of impending death. But the conscious mind refused to accept the signal. In those days I felt a helplessness I had never felt before. Even today, none of us who knew him really have the solace of knowing that we had done all that we could, because of the simple reason that none of us really knew what to do. Medical science had failed. The rational mind refused to look for other avenues.

I do not have any logical explanation for what I have felt. I only wish that I knew how to help him. I only wish that some day I gain the abilities and power to counter such a shadow. Death will come when it will, but I cannot accept losing someone just because we have not learnt to cope with dangers and afflictions of another dimension.

It is easy enough to rationalise about the cause of any death. There is always an apparent cause. Almost all death certificates narrate death as having been caused by 'respiratory failure'. That is always the immediate cause, but the real cause is almost always, something else.

To me, this death of a very dear one has again exposed the limitations of our thinking process, our knowledge and perceptions. Death comes up in so many ways that let alone the understanding we do not even get to know the various forms it can take.

Life has thrown up yet another challenge, which has to be met – although I do not know how.

Maybe through death, life has posed a question, the answer to which I cannot perceive yet!

Death comes up in so many ways that let alone the understanding we do not even get to know the various forms it can take.

*We did not change as we grew older; we just became more clearly ourselves." - Lynn Hall*

# Friendship

There were almost 300 people in the hall. My friend was reading the article he had authored and I was crying. Nobody saw me, but nevertheless I was crying.

It was an article on friendship, a paper, which had been given an award and would be presented at the forthcoming convention. What was special was that the paper mentioned me. It mentioned that the author had learnt everything about friendship from the 35 years of friendship that he shared with me.

It made me delve into my own feelings and examine what our friendship was all about and what it had all meant to me. In so many ways I knew that I had failed him. Was I always there when he really needed me – Not really! On a personal level he went through hell at one point, but there was little that I did or could do.

What made the event more poignant was the fact that for the past one year, our friendship was passing through a very critical phase. Critical it was in every sense of the word. I had been very harsh with him in our professional dealings. Apart from being friends we were professional colleagues and partners in a Consulting venture. Lately, I had been merciless in my efforts to make him rise to what I perceived were the standards necessary to reach the targets we had set ourselves. Those were not easy times. Any weaker relationship would not have been able to withstand the onslaught brought about by me.

But it also told me that our friendship had passed a very critical stage of growth. It is only when you can criticize without any fear of being misunderstood and without generating any ill-will that you finally know that yours is a strong friendship. It is only when you can work on each other's faults that your friendship can be called mature. He had taken all of it from me gamely. Maybe not agreeing all the time, but trusting my intent all the same.

As I sat there, quietly shedding tears, I realised that it calls for tremendous understanding to take criticism, harshness and fault finding in your stride. It calls for a deep level trust to know that what a friend is doing is totally in your interests.

I am lucky to have a friend who had all this. He in turn has given these important insights into friendship.

My tears were my thanks and tribute to the friendship that I have shared with him.

It calls for a deep level trust to know that what a friend is doing is totally in your interests.

*"Sometimes we must get hurt in order to grow. We must fail in order to know. Sometimes our vision is clear only after our eyes are washed away with tears."*
*– Unknown*

# Maa

A part of me has gone with her.

From that small little room in that Haveli (*old fashioned private mansion*) in a remote town of Rajasthan where she bore me, to the bustling metropolis of Kolkata that she made her home, I could always feel the umbilical chord – the emotional tug as well as the physical presence of it. I still walk, what I felt as a child were a few miles, from the well to home, through those dusty lanes, holding her hand as she balanced a few pitchers on her head and held yet another on to her waist with the other hand. I still remember her wail which I hated and yet heard every time she parted from my maternal home.

And was it just my imagination that every morsel she fed me had an unparalleled taste, that every time she caressed me when I was unwell made me feel better, that her lap was the most secure place on earth? It may be imagination for the world, but to me it is every bit true as the sun I felt this morning – as true as her departure from the world as we know it.

The last three months of her life we struggled hard to save her. But it was not to be. She remained in considerable pain throughout this time. The last 15 days were far worse when she was conscious only in bits and pieces. And I would hear the usual clichés about how 'her suffering should now end'. But it was this period, which made me realize what she meant to me. It was this period, which brought my entire mental focus on to her.

This was the phase of my life where nothing else mattered – only she existed. Perhaps in a way I was feeling something close to what she must have felt when I was born. In some small way I could get a glimpse of the motherly love that she showered on me all her life.

Like most parents at her age she had reached a stage in life where she was perhaps beginning to believe that she mattered little to her children now, that priorities of her children lay with their own children. Life gave me and my sister, an opportunity to show her how much she meant to us – how much we loved her. In spite of her pain this renewed realization gave her more happiness than we could imagine. If that does not lend a meaning to suffering what does? I do believe once that happened she may have been in pain but she no longer suffered.

It is only at such times that you become aware of the sterling qualities of the loved one you are about to lose. No matter how little she had, she had always given. If ever she asked me for money it was only to give in my name & for my benefit. I only pray that something of this quality would remain with me.

But I do know that in some ways, a part of her will always remain with me.

And I would hear the usual clichés about how 'her suffering should now end'. But it was this period, which made me realize what she meant to me. It was this period, which brought my entire mental focus on to her.

*"If we will be quiet and ready enough, we shall find compensation in every disappointment."*
*–Henry David Thoreau*

# Compensation

There are no blank spaces – when you lose something, you gain something else

So many times in life I have had the feeling of tremendous loss! Whether it was the loss of a friend, an opportunity, a job, an asset, money or a feeling – each loss felt like a setback at that point of time. That loss seemed permanent and irreparable. It seemed that nothing on earth could ever replace it.

But in time something else comes along. Not to really replace it. Something else altogether, something apparently unconnected.... and yet somehow deeply related. Life always has its own ways to compensate us. There are no blank spaces. It may take its own time to happen or it may take its own time for us to recognize that compensation. But life never scrounges – it is always generous with its compensation.

> There are no blank spaces – when you lose something, you gain something else

*"When we strive to become better than we are,*
*everything around us becomes better too."*
*–Paulo Coelho*

# Grandma

Ever since I can remember she loved me. She loved me without conditions. No matter what the issue she was always there to side with me. Amongst all my cousins if there was anyone who was always granted favours by her, it was I.

I can recollect innumerable instances when she tucked away sweets for me – away from the prying eyes of the dozens of members of the household. I would spend hours reading out the 'Ramayana' to her. (At least it seemed like hours then). As a child I knew that I had an unshakable ally in her no matter what took place. The most tender touch, I have ever felt was that of her loving hand on my brow, when I was aching all over with fever. All my life I received nothing but love from her.

But as I grew up, I stopped seeing love and saw more of her orthodoxy & irrational beliefs. Slowly but surely, I started opposing, what I believed, to be her blind faith. Her eccentricities became the butt of my ridicule. Most of the time the banter was light hearted but sometimes it was dead serious. But her attitude remained unchanged. She still remained as loving as ever – always supportive, always by my side. In so many ways I was too immature to understand her love. Like all growing youngsters I was busy with my own world, full of my own sense of righteousness; too preoccupied with my immediate surroundings to even notice the important aspects of life like love.

When her end came she used to live with us. We slept in the same room. For more than six months she suffered as her kidneys failed. She became delirious in her toxic ridden state. She would keep rambling on, asking for something or the other. And I, who had received nothing but love from her, had, more often than not, nothing to give her except my irritated responses. Night after night of disturbance roused my ire. To the extent, that one night, I muttered "Why doesn't she die?"... although I did not really mean them, I did utter those words.

Indeed, she did not live very long in that state. One afternoon, right in front of my eyes she passed away. She was not in her senses for the last few days of her life. Although, we were expecting the inevitable, I was really sad. But I never fully realised what I had lost.

Years passed. But somewhere inside me there was the guilt of having wronged her. Somewhere inside me I had not forgiven myself for not even acknowledging her unconditional love. So what if she was not a perfect human being. Who is?

Life gave me an opportunity to admit my shame, to come to terms with it. I was fortunate enough to be able to do it. Perhaps that opened up a doorway, which had remained closed for so long. Soon after that I went through the toughest part of my life. It was an emotionally terrifying phase. In those frightening hours of my life, I felt she had come back. I felt her love again. In those months when I felt terribly alone, I felt her presence with me. I almost felt that tender touch.

Through that phase of my life, I came to know how lucky I had been, to receive the kind of love that I had received. In the darkest hour of my life I found one of the brightest spots of my life. I found the strength of love. It was her love, which made me feel wanted.

I found my own worth through the grandmother I had lost long ago. I found her again, this time for keeps. For I know that her love is as much a part of me, as the flesh and bones in my body are.

Somewhere inside me I had not forgiven myself for not even acknowledging her unconditional love. So what if she was not a perfect human being. Who is?

*"Civilization is the progress toward*
*a society of privacy.*
*The savage's whole existence is public,*
*ruled by the laws of his tribe.*
*Civilization is the process of setting man free from*
*men." –Ayn Rand*

# The Other Kind of Progress

More & more we tend to measure the progress of people by their material success, advancement in technology and economic vibrancy. But then is it all that there is to being human? It is quite possible that there may exist civilizations which have developed a deep level of understanding of the human mind, where people can communicate without speaking;

...where one person can reach out and heal the hurt of another without lifting a hand or using the laser;

...where the evolution of the spirit is the yardstick of progress and material progress is the fallout of that evolution rather than standing on the crushed remains of human spirit;

...where power is defined by the ability to heal and not by the capability of detonating nuclear devices;

...where reality is not taken to be only what you can see, touch & feel;

...where the spirit is perceived beyond physics!

The day we find this world perhaps we'll also realize what we have lost from the period we call ancient history...the world that could have been!

Perhaps we'll also see it as the world that may have been ours!!

More & more we tend to measure the progress of people by their material success, advancement in technology and economic vibrancy. But then is it all that there is to being human?

*A bird does not sing because it has an answer.*
*It sings because it has a song. – Chinese Proverb*

# Daughter

The stereotype images associated with attaining fatherhood are – jumping with joy, going completely ballistic, running around and telling everyone of the great news.

I didn't act in any such manner. Nor did I feel overwhelmed at that moment. For me it was quite an un-dramatic moment. Fatherhood took its own time to sink into me. As my daughter started growing up in to an angelic doll she started to grow into my life and mind.

Without my realizing it, I was slowly and surreptitiously transformed into a doting father. By the time she reached her first birthday I was completely under her spell (I still am). Just seeing her would fill me with sheer joy. Even today her angelic face with that endearing smile is etched so clearly into my heart. There was something in her which drew love from everyone who came in touch with her. I suppose it was simply because she was so generous with her own love.

To this day she has that uncanny ability to brighten up her surroundings. I have sometimes wondered what makes her so special. And special she is – not because she is my daughter but because she has what the French call 'joie de vivre' – the joy of living. She is in every moment of her life with every cell of her being.

It is through her life has taught me the meaning of love & joy. I have seen & experienced the exultation of spirit. That by itself makes life so meaningful. My Maker has shown HIS love for me by sending me this unbelievably precious gift.

I suppose this is why I did not feel that temporary joy when she came into my life. After all she had come as a lasting happiness...and as a source of solace for my own spirit.

There was something in her which drew love from everyone who came in touch with her. I suppose it was simply because she was so generous with her own love.

*Intelligence should not be confused with wisdom.*
*There are many highly intelligent*
*fools in the world, who use their intellects*
*to justify, not to eliminate,their delusion.*
*–Omar Khayyam's Rubaiyat*

# The Foolish use of Intelligence

Mankind was blessed with intelligence, but sometimes I wonder whether it is an unmixed blessing. It is amazing to see how we use this very intelligence to hold on to silly perceptions. How we have allowed our obsessions with the sensory perceptions and rational thinking to dominate our lives and world-views. How we have stopped ourselves from developing newer levels of awareness and higher ways of thinking.

The room where I am sitting, the very house itself and the city along with it, is rotating at thousands of miles an hour. It is not only rotating, it is hurtling through space at a speed of millions of miles an hour. Billions of particles are passing right through us and all that we see around us, on their way to the far distant galaxies. We can perceive none of this. The world we see is so very different from what the other creatures see. We can see such a short band on the light spectrum and are blind to the rest .... and yet we have the impertinence to assert that what WE perceive IS the reality.

As man has delved into the sub atomic world he has realized that nature has blocked our access to the essential nature of things through the sense organs. The first lesson that the new science learnt was that senses are not of much use in this search for the 'basic building blocks' of the universe. ... And yet intelligent men, smug in their knowledge keep telling us to believe only in our senses of perception. **The message given out by the society is that anyone who talks about going beyond the senses has taken leave of his senses.**

Quantum physics, which has made amazing journey into the sub-atomic world, has established that the existence of matter on its own, has no meaning; that this is not a world of isolated matter, it is a world of interconnected events. An objective description of the world is no longer valid. ..... And yet we have been conditioned into believing that only the tangible is real.

The new Science has established that elementary 'forces' in the universe work instantly across time & space ......and yet we disbelieve any healing methods which use the universal life force because they defy the barriers of time & space!

The lesser known discoveries of science indicate that any event happening anywhere in the universes has a deep interconnection with any other happening in any other part of the universe. There is a basic unity in the cosmos with every part being linked to its environment. .....and yet for 'scientific' minded people it unfashionable to believe that stars and galaxies far away can exert any influence on the happenings on earth.

The very basic concepts of time, space & causation which mankind has held on to, for thousands of years have totally lost their validity. Higher science has confirmed that there has to be a shift in awareness if we are to have any understanding of the nature of this universe of ours....and yet the major chunk of mankind likes to believe that that the logic we cannot comprehend is a logic that cannot exist.

As science gets wiser this universe seems more like an organic being, pulsating and moving with happenings and not things. Every part, right from our deepest desires to the farthest blinking quasar is connected to the other, in one way or the other and this connection goes beyond time and space. There is no existence of any material substance. All existence only seems to exist as an activity of the elementary energy, which takes the shapes and forms of substances and forces.

This is the wonder and mystery of this wonderful universe.

With the fundamental world-view having undergone such a drastic transformation it is amazing that the intelligent man still takes the refuge of the classical science and continues to...

....deny all that is subtle and intangible

....deny all that heals without chemicals.

....deny all that crosses the boundary of time & space

....deny all that he cannot touch and see.

....deny all that is beyond logic

and still thinks of himself as a man with a scientific attitude.

It is precisely because of this 'scientific' attitude that we perhaps get a Newton or an Einstein once in a blue moon.

It seems that for thousands of years the majority of human beings have been using, one part of the brain and managed to totally subdue the other. The rational half of our brain has totally stifled the creative half of our brain. As a result creativity and art have suffered and lots of systems and knowledge have virtually disappeared or can only be found under 'cult' labels.

Skepticism is a healthy use of intelligence but cynicism and that too with a conditioned mind is a sure sign of decay. There seems to be too much of intelligence in the world and too little of wonder &

magic. If this magic is to unfold we must teach our intelligence to watch and experience rather than to judge and condemn with a deluded mind.

We need a lot more sense of wonder in our approach towards life which is the hallmark of scientific thinking ….not the 'I know it all' attitude of the intelligent ignoramus.

As individuals also, the magic in our lives can unfold only if we have an attitude which is open to possibilities… when we take the universe for granted we also make our lives dull.

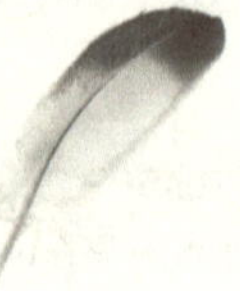

There is no existence of any material substance. All existence only seems to exist as an activity of the elementary energy, which takes the shapes and forms of substances and forces.

*"The happiest people don't have the best of everything. They just make the best of everything that they have. Live simply. Love generously. Care deeply. Speak kindly. And enjoy your hot chocolate"*

# Much is required from those who are given much

What do you call a person who is always full of life and exuding zest; bubbling with laughter and cheer. A person who is free with her love...who bares her soul to you and engulfs you with her affection.

She is not my sister and yet she is that and much more than that. I have virtually seen her grow up. Even when she was a small child I saw the same qualities in her. She is more than a decade younger to me and yet there developed a bond between us which bridges this gap. Perhaps it was this liveliness which pulled me towards her and in spite of our age gap we reached out so effortlessly and spontaneously. Over the years I came closer to her. It is not that I could meet her very often but there was a genuine warmth and concern for each other. Even as a youngster I wished she would get a suitable match as a life partner for her who deserved her, for she was very special to me.

I had never met anyone who was so spontaneous in giving love.... always full of life.... always full of bubbles. I would always feel upbeat when I met her. She always made me want to protect her. It seems odd but these intangible qualities in her always made me feel she was God's special one. To me, she epitomizes love. As I describe her, nothing but these qualities, come to the mind. Maybe because in essence, this is what she is all about! Perhaps because of these qualities she never lacked friends and admirers. She always used to be surrounded by friends, basking in all the attention she got throughout her childhood right to the time she got married.

But life always demands something more out of the gifted ones. In fact it demands a lot more from its favourite children.....its children who symbolize what living is all about. So she had to face the most difficult test of life through marriage. The person who had received love constantly from the people around her suddenly found herself in a household and surroundings where no one had any love to give. She was now amongst persons who had been starved of love. Her new relations could only rebuff love. To them love was alien and frightening and they reacted with emotional cruelty.

Her new world was just the opposite of what I had hoped for her. To most people she had nothing to complain about. Wealth, social standing, status – she had everything – what more could she ask for. But what about what she was? Her surroundings were tough by any standards and more so for her. Her real world was quite different from what was perceived by people….the world where people actually live – the world of feelings.

The girl who was brought up on love, the girl who lived to love was suddenly starved of love.

Then I gradually saw her bubbles dissipate. The eyes in which I always saw laughter and life reflected pain now. Her growing up in the cynical world had begun. She had a lot to learn. She has fought gamely…. fought for her dignity, for her peace and for her right to be loved and struggled to reach her womanhood. But more than anything else it has been a battle between the 'stream' that she is and the 'desert', which surrounds her.

To me it is the ultimate test of her being. She was gifted and gifted abundantly with love. But I suppose it was with a purpose. She was perhaps meant to reach a place where she was needed the most. This love stream was meant to go through a desert. She has been put to the ultimate test. Does she have enough love in her to revive the people who surround her life! I believe she does. And I think I can only help her by becoming stronger. She would have to fight her own battles but she would need all the strength that perhaps I or anyone else who loves her can give her. My love can be a reminder to her of the wealth of love in her. It may help her remain what she essentially is. I want to ensure that.

I suppose she faces the ultimate test of love. To love in spite of not finding love around you....to rediscover love as a verb. I do see a few bushes in the desert around her now. To me this is proof that she has indeed made progress. The desert may never become a forest, but then it was never meant to be. What matters, is that the stream must never dry up! I know it won't, for I have seen the source. There are times when I look into her eyes and perceive her soul. I can still see those bubbles. The stream is alive and well.

Her real world was quite different from what was perceived by people....the world where people actually live – the world of feelings.

*"That which does not kill us makes us stronger." – Friedrich Nietzsche*

# What maketh the Strong!

What makes strong people strong? What is it that gives them strength? ... a strength to look anyone in the eye. Obviously I do not refer to the physical strength here. I mean the mental strength; the moral strength; the strength to bear hardship and not lose oneself; the fortitude and the strength of character

I also do not refer to what generally passes of as strength. What we generally perceive as strength is merely an act - a bluff. There are apparently strong persons bluffing their way through life. They indulge in bluster and manage to impress people with their apparent confidence.

You will find such kind all around you. They occupy senior positions in a lot of Institutions; they have seen success, they have risen in life; they seem to be the life of any party with their put-on bonhomie – politics is full of them. But such people are very insecure. They are busy exercising their powers over people who cannot retaliate. They are cruel because they are weak. They are always envious of the genuinely confident people for they know that their own success is undeserved - it has been built upon the exploitation of others. They are aware that they have bluffed their way through life.

Then there are the weak ones who are always in a huge majority. They are weak and obviously so. They try to get around by getting in good books of the tyrants through flattery & sycophancy. They always shy away from facing life. Escapism is their mantra for getting through life. Responsibility is an anathema. In their book, principles are for fools.

And then there are the people with real strength. The strong ones are the ones to whom everyone flocks when they are in trouble, when they are down, when they need help& when they need succor. They act as pillars and they also act as lighthouses.

But how do these people become so strong? They are not necessarily wealthy nor are they very influential. They do not walk the corridors of power & they do not hobnob with the celebrities. They do not have a great social standing nor are they necessarily intellectuals.

Their source of strength actually lies in their ability to be in touch with their deeper self. The real strength comes only to those who dare to do the right things and do not opt for the easy way. They have always paid the price. They have not gone for free lunches in life. They listen to that inner voice and do not heed the cunning intelligence. They do not try to win by defeating others.

It is this choice of taking the right way over taking the easy way which makes all the difference. A clean conscience is their source of power & strength.

When you think of strength of character, you think of people like MK Gandhi, Martin Luther King, Nelson Mandela, Abraham Lincoln, Suu Kyi.. and so on...

But then what was it that made them different? To my mind, when you refuse to take the easy way you invest in your character. But when you compromise you lose a bit of yourself and no amount of material success in life can replenish it.

When you always treat people fairly, justly & compassionately you become a beacon which attracts human beings.

When you face hardship you actually invest in your character. That is the time which is building your strength – that is when your inner steel gets tempered. There CAN be no short cut when it comes to forming character.

If I feel inadequate or weak the only reason can be that I have not been true to my conscience – I have chosen the easy way out in most situations. I have been scared of choosing the right way because it seemed difficult.

I also need to ask myself who have I treated unfairly, when I didn't do the right thing, when did I ignore the voice of my conscience.... for the key to being strong is doing right!

It is only then that I can look in the eyes of the 'Guy in the Glass' without flinching and that would be the ultimate test of character! THAT would be strength!

When you refuse to take the easy way you invest in your character. But when you compromise you lose a bit of yourself and no amount of material success in life can replenish it.

*There is but one success - to be able to spend your life in your own way."*
*– Christopher Morley*

# Can I ever live up to it?

"You have been my idol since childhood"

The words shook me up. As the train pulled out of the station, I stood on the platform with that little slip of paper in my hand – words that conveyed love, trust and a deep connection. These words had been written by someone who had been a friend and a younger brother to me for the last decade or so. A brother I never had and yet always had in him. I just stood rooted to the spot in the middle of the hustle & bustle. Time just stood still. So many years of warmth, friendship & togetherness just flashed before my eyes.

It was 1980. B... was leaving for Bombay as his father had been transferred and I had just seen him off. We said our good-byes and just before boarding the train, he handed me a small slip of paper and told me to read it only after he had left. I knew he was leaving Calcutta for good. Life had changed for all of us. The carefree days were coming to an end. Higher studies and careers beckoned to all of us. The childhood full of comics of TinTin, Superman & Commando; novels of Alistair Maclean, Agatha Christie & Louis L'amour; movies of Clint Eastwood, Trinity & Amitabh Bachchan and the evenings spent playing Badminton & Table Tennis had slid into the past even before we could realize that we were living the most spontaneous days of our lives.

Actually I was his elder brother's age group. But perhaps there was something deeper which brought us closer. There was something subtle we shared, something which went beyond the apparent relationship, something, which somehow crossed the 5 yr age difference. I became one of his closest friends and yet remained like an elder brother as well. The love of Wild West, the books of SUDDEN, the stories of Louis L'amour and good food were things we both were passionate about. I loved his sense of humour and the knack of coming up with the most apt *Sheir (urdu couplets)* on many an occasion. We would spend hours together just reading – there was no need to talk. But beyond all that I loved his shayari. As he grew older this knack grew. But the strangest part was that his unique talents were unknown to most people. Most such things he was comfortable sharing only with me and a few other people.

The real B... was well hidden. He would always withdraw in the company of strangers. He made few friends, but when made friends he went all the way. Perhaps it was shyness that prevented him from pursuing his passion. What made him so special? I don't think I have come across a more guileless person. His simplicity & innocence was almost other worldly.

But I always felt that somewhere deep down there was a sadness within him. Perhaps it stemmed from the fact that he could not pursue his calling. What exactly that was, I do not know! To me it always appeared that he was a reluctant Marine Engineer. In one of his letters to me he bared his soul when he wrote:

*Saagar ki maujon se ye paigam aaya hai*
*Ek badnaseeb shayar ka salaam aaya hai*
*[the waves of the ocean carry a message;*
*salutations come from a poet who is ill fated]*

I always felt he was a lonely sailor. Only managing to connect with a few people he felt were sensitive enough and understood him. If he found me with other company he would generally prefer to come back some other time. In some ways he was not at ease with a world not very willing to understand him.

I understood him. But how often do people understand persons like him. Somewhere down the line, a lot of individuals find themselves living someone else's life. Perhaps it is in the scheme of things that we lose such people so early. His purity & innocence is what I am always reminded of, whenever I think of him:

*Tar damini pe sheikh hamari na jaiye*
*Daaman nichod dein to farishte wazoo karein*
*[Wet may be my garment, do not be misled by it*
*As holy water would Angels treat it, were I to wring it]*

For the past two years I thought of him more often than not. I talked to him as often as I could. I visited him more often than I ever had, because for the past two years I had known that time was running out; because for the past two years he had been battling blood cancer. But there was not once that I saw any pessimism in his outlook. I always found him with a smile and hope. The last time I saw him was when I turned to look back as I closed the door of the hospital room. He sat looking at me with a smile and gave me a 'thumbs up'.

He is gone at just 45, leaving a hole in the lives of people who loved him. I think the only reason he came into this world was to keep reminding us that nothing is more important than just being human.

May I get the strength and ability to live up to his expectations!

May both of us find friendship in all our sojourns into this world and the worlds beyond!

> I think the only reason he came into this world was to keep reminding us that nothing is more important than just being human.

*"We must let go of the life we planned, so as to accept the one that is waiting for us."*

## Freedom

How I long for more freedom! Somehow I do not measure success or achievement in terms of money acquired or fame earned. I know that I would be completely content when, whatever I have done or achieved, gives me the kind of freedom I want.

More & more I feel a pang of longing to be there in those beautiful cozy corners in different parts of the world – be it a small cottage in the hilly Switzerland, a street café in France, that white strip of beach in Bali surrounded by the crystal clear aquamarine water, that log cabin on the side of the gurgling river in Manali, that table beside that white fencing or that wood paneled corner in that warm restaurant – there are so many places that still beckon to me.

I want to be on that terrace overlooking the ocean with somebody playing the saxophone in the night – the cool ocean breeze blowing gently across. I want to see those ancient pyramids and hear the past talk to me. I want to look down the Grand Canyon and I also want to see the remnants of the Incan civilization deep in the deserts of the Wild West.

I want to visit the remnants of the pre-historic and ancient Vedic civilization, the remains of which are scattered across India along the erstwhile Saraswati river. I really long to be in those places, with people I love, with friends who understand not only my words but also my silences.

With this longing has also come a realization that there are lots of such moments and corners which are around and only need to be availed of. That is what they mean perhaps when they say that you must 'smell the roses on the way'. I have postponed that breakfast outing for too long - no more - if I can't afford that expensive corner I shall find another, for, the right corner for that moment which I deserve, at this point in time, is always there, I just need to be more aware.

I want to see those ancient pyramids and hear the past talk to me. I want to look down the Grand Canyon and I also want to see the remnants of the Incan civilization deep in the deserts of the Wild West.

*"Take care of all your memories. For you cannot relive them." – Bob Dylan*

# The Recapturing of Memory Lanes

How I wish I had a memory like that of some of my friends. Was I not paying attention and savouring those moments? Must be so, otherwise I would not have lost track of such large parts of my life's moments! Or is it that I have been too engrossed with stress of the struggle of existence. Either way, I feel I have lost much that is precious and yet at one level I know it is all retrievable, I only have to reach the center of being where time has not been able to make a dent.

Sometimes I try and retrieve some of what I have lost by making some nostalgic visits. They are all there inside me somewhere - the house which belongs to my childhood; the hill station where

I spent that vacation; the space where a building full of memories stood; the town where I spent my childhood; the classroom where I sat as a kid learning my first lessons - and they all seem to call me, they are my faint links to a world which beckons through a ghostly mist... a world which now seems to stand in another dimension.

That small town I was born in still pulls me, so does the old haveli where my mother was brought up and where I spent some of my childhood. It seemed so huge then. With every visit of mine, after an interval of a few years, it seemed to shrink. In spite of the dirt and the squalor I wanted to enter that unkempt haveli and the room I was born in. During a recent visit, I showed it to my kids and their joy and wonder was also a treat to watch. But I do not know what I kept looking for, what I kept trying to recapture - was it the people who were so much a part of that place, was it their presence I longed for? There was sadness too for all that had changed.

I kept looking for all that that had not changed.

There are so many such places - those are my pilgrimages and my visits are a homage to the people who were there and still are a part of me.

Futile? Maybe! But it does bring back some of those human and material links and some kind of chain forms again. And some part of my heart is fulfilled; some part of me feels rested - as if a debt has been paid.

But I do not know what I kept looking for, what I kept trying to recapture - was it the people who were so much a part of that place, was it their presence I longed for? There was sadness too for all that had changed.

*"I am only one, but still I am one. I cannot do everything, but still I can do something; and because I cannot do everything, I will not refuse to do something that I can do."*

# Healing the Hurt of Others

Sometimes I wish I had the emotional maturity, confidence and spontaneity earlier in my life. Had it been so I would not have regretted those moments when I could not reach out, comfort and heal some of the people who came in my life.

How can I forget the face of B___ di, who lay there dying of cancer. A couple of months before her death I sat by her bedside. She spoke that day, although she was never very eloquent. She spoke of people who came to comfort her and spoke of spirituality and reading religious books or God's word as they put it. Everybody seemed to have the same thing to say - how she should be preparing for the next world, what she should be reading - all of them trying to intellectualize about her suffering and loneliness. As if on a cue, I asked her whether at times she didn't really need and wish for a loving hand on her head, a person who just came to give her love and emotional support? The moment I spoke of it, she nodded her head vigorously in agreement and broke into sobs uncontrollably. I had touched a raw nerve. This brave woman was also human and needed love, more than anything else in the world. Sermons were no substitute for love. But I too, sat there like a fool - understanding her need but not having courage or confidence to reach out to her and heal her emotional pain.

Many a times, after that I have reached out in my mind towards her and held her close, gently stroking her head. But that actual moment passed and I lost it. I just couldn't bring myself around to do it when it was needed. Sometime later she passed away and when I heard the news that moment I had shared with her is what I saw in my mind. I again felt her emotional pain - a pain which I could have tried to heal, but did not have the courage or maturity to deal with.

In some solemn moments I relive that moment wishing and visualizing that I AM actually reaching out to her and healing that hurt, when no one thought of that little girl inside the paralyzed woman's body.....that little girl who just wanted to be hugged and told that she was loved. Why don't people like us have the courage to come out with our emotions, to say that we love our friends and near and dear ones, especially when they need it the most?

Why do we act as if by ignoring something, it will disappear?

Is this casual approach a defense mechanism?

I do understand now that the expressions of our deepest feelings and love have the power to heal.

I hope that one lost moment in life has given me strength enough to deal with the hurt of others. If it has, I would certainly be able to make a difference in the lives of at least some people on this planet.

Why don't people like us have the courage to come out with our emotions, to say that we love our friends and near and dear ones, especially when they need it the most?

*"The ultimate reason for setting goals is to entice you to become the person it takes to achieve them." – Jim Rohn*

# Romancing the Sand

Dawn was breaking as I stood in the open gate of the train compartment. As far as I could see there were sand dunes all around. The land in Rajasthan was pockmarked with scraggy misshapen trees which looked battle scarred and ageless. The train bounced on the small gauge tracks forcing me to hold on tightly to the handle bars at the gate. The speed of the train lifted the sand and it swirled all around but it didn't bother me for it was so very clean. There was stillness in the landscape. There was nobody to be seen for miles around.

And I simply loved it.

The desert has always held a deep and tremendous attraction for me. The next few days were fascinating. The boundaries of our farm I had gone to visit, simply merged into the land all around. Some part of me merged into that land.

The swirling sandstorms, the vast distances, those deformed trees, that uncanny silence - all of these became a part of me. And with this intermingling started the formation of a dream - the dream of an oasis in the middle of this barren land. I worked for this dream for a long time - planting hundreds of trees, staying in that small town for weeks on end, hundreds of miles away from my home.

And yet there was danger and torment in that land too. For plants would not survive the heat, those which, survived, would be destroyed by the termite. And the termite....which nothing could destroy. And yet life survived all around. With the slightest bit of moisture life would sprout all around showing its dormant power and presence all around. In that wilderness I also felt the presence of things which did not belong to our realm. I heard such things. I saw such things. I also felt the palpable faith of the people of that land.

Every trip to that area brought me in touch with something new and fascinating. It also brought me in touch with myself. That land always did exist somewhere deep inside me .... perhaps that is why it called me there, with no apparent rhyme or reason. I had never thought I would give up a job and start raising plants in the middle of nowhere. But it did happen.

I worked on the project for years. I lost heavily in terms of money and effort over those years. The project itself was ahead of its time and beyond my resources. Yet it did not really matter, for as I look back I can see that it was not really about the project. I realize now, it wasn't a project – it was a romance. At times our lives are shaped by our simple love for some things or people. Our lives are shaped by the small things, which drive us. It is not the big things that drive us. We are driven by the primal emotions – whether positive or negative.

Emotions like anger, love, jealousy, hatred, passion drive most people to heights or depths. The world may find lofty reasons or ideologies behind the achievements or crimes; but scratch a little deeper and most of the times you will find simple human feelings shaping a person's destiny.

In some measure and to some extent, a period of my life was shaped by my love for the desert.

At times our lives are shaped by our simple love for some things or people. Our lives are shaped by the small things, which drive us. It is not the big things that drive us. We are driven by the primal emotions – whether positive or negative.

*"Character cannot be developed in ease and quiet. Only through experience of trial and suffering can the soul be strengthened, ambition inspired, and success achieved."*

# Have I lost much?

Time and again I trusted... depended on people. Time and again, I was let down, that too by people whom I taught, to whom I gave unconditionally, who swore by me, who were there with me when the going was good. And when they thought they would make a killing or they would get an advantage they chose to betray me. I am not bitter, for, I was not fooled. I was betrayed.

There is so much I lost in material terms because I chose to trust. But that is not what hurts. What hurts is the fact that I could not read them properly.... Did I go wrong, somewhere?

Should I stop trusting? I don't think that I ever will. Why should I stop being myself? I shall be trusting ... for life means trusting and trust is a part of me. Why should I allow someone else to decide what I shall be.... What I shall do ... what shall be my guiding principle in my life. Am I bitter? I don't think so. Today, I can only pity the people, who have been untrustworthy, for they will find it difficult to live with themselves. They will never have the courage to look me in the eye. They will always have something to hide. It is not in me, to hate ... it is such a wasted emotion. They are the ones who will have to live with what they did. Isn't that punishment!

Have I lost much? I don't think so, because the last ten years of my life have given me wonderful experiences. They are wonderful for I have chosen to learn from them. The breach of trust has also made me that much stronger. I have not lost much because all that matters in life is still with me. All that really makes life worthwhile cannot be taken away... and the ability, confidence and courage to trust is one such thing. So why should I stop trusting! It is not that I was gullible...but there must have been a purpose to what happened and why it happened.

All this taught me something. Yes, it has. It has taught me that I must become someone in life whom no one would ever want to betray. I must become so strong as to ensure that the good would respect me enough and the bad would fear me enough. The tough part in me and the good part in me must coexist and should be evident to the people who come in touch with me. Toughness must be an essential ingredient of being good.

Good need not mean being soft.

The meek shall inherit the earth? Sure.... because it means without ego... not without strength!

The tough part in me and the good part in me must coexist and should be evident to the people who come in touch with me. Toughness must be an essential ingredient of being good.

*"A man who limits his interests, limits his life."*
*–Vincent Price*

# The Man who wanted too much

What is it that makes me want more out of each moment! No – I have never had greed. Never have I hankered for riches I did not deserve. Ambition I have always had.... the ambition to do something – ambition to become something, but never in the sense of acquiring and possessing. I know the rewards would come in due course. And yet, I have also been very keen to get more out of every moment – out of every relationship.

Isn't life all about living to the full? If I do not fully get what each moment, each event, each person has to offer or has the potential to offer. Am I not letting life drift by?

I know for sure....it would have been a crime, not to savour that delicacy in Lucknow. I would have missed something had I not stopped and listened to the haunting melodies of the violinist on the street that night. I would have never known that dimension in my friend had I not listened intently to the expression of his feelings. I would have missed my daughter's talent if I had not paid attention to her humming. The beautiful sight of the lit-up dunes on the golf course would not have been with me had I not been aware in a moment when other things were screaming for my attention.

Where is living to the hilt, if I just pass through all that socializing, vacationing & working without really drinking in each moment, enjoying each mind that I come across, admiring every beautiful person or thing that touches my life! What is the point of celebrating a festival if its spirit, significance and feeling is not captured? Do we really celebrate a festival or an occasion or do we really go through the same thing on every different occasion – that is what we need to ask ourselves.

If we can get engrossed in the meaning of every happening or event it is bound to arouse different emotions and is bound to remain a treasure we shall cherish. I suppose that is the reason why most of us are unable to remember most occasions – because we never made them significant – never wanted more out of them.

Am I wrong in wanting that much out of life? I do want to draw out the significance of each special day – be it someone's birthday, anniversary or a festival. And I do tend to get disappointed when people around do not show the same degree of enthusiasm. The tragedy has been that a lot of times

I do not express all this myself in the apprehension of not being understood. And I too end up looking deflated and unenthusiastic in a few situations. I haven't done justice to living myself.

Do I push people too much or make them uncomfortable when I want more of them....? I do know most people live only a part of what they really are and when I find that I do share some rapport, I want to draw that person out. I want to draw out whatever he or she really is, rather than go through the rigmarole and sham of socialising. There is that suppressed laughter that I want to hear. There is that smile which lights up the eyes that I want to see. There is the joy of singing that I want to hear in that voice. There is that real face behind every mask that I want to see.

In the process I have perhaps pushed some relationships hard. Sometimes I have wanted to drag along with me the persons I wanted to be with. I have wanted them to be with me in places and times where we could all be expressing all that living is all about. I have wanted to turn around and say 'Hey, isn't that beautiful!" But most times I find I am unable to stretch them so far. Why is that so? This kind of sharing is not an ordinary sharing for me. This is what enlivening life is all about. But everyone is so taken up by all that is mundane. For most people a vacation is just a vacation, an outing is just an outing, a meal is just a meal, a beach is just a beach, a song is just a song. But to me it is so much more than that and that is what I want to convey to the ones I care to be with. But nobody seems to have time for all this.

I suppose I would have to take a lot more initiative to make every significant occasion a little more memorable – a little more special for all my near and dear ones. If I want a lot more out of life I will have to go out and give a lot more. It is then perhaps that I would be able to draw people out and make them live. It is then perhaps that I would be able to live more of myself. At times it becomes so difficult. How do I explain all this? How many will understand? Really!!!! Do I want too much out of life? Or is it that people are satisfied with too little?

If I want a lot more out of life I will have to go out and give a lot more. It is then perhaps that I would be able to draw people out and make them live. It is then perhaps that I would be able to live more of myself.

*"Destiny isn't determined by chance, but rather by the choices that chance gives..." – Unknown*

## Awareness

As I turned the corner I smelt them. The smell of those flowers brought back awareness with a jolt. I had not smelt these flowers for more than two years. It was amazing because for more than thirty years this smell always held significance for me. I had never missed it. It always meant the coming festivities, fun frolic and holidays. This was one of the smells, which made me feel it was good to be alive. But then something had gone wrong. I had stopped smelling these flowers.

The season came and went. But my awareness was not there. I must have passed those flowers so many times during the same season in the last two years also. But for me – they did not exist.

It is only now that I can see it clearly. I had stopped living. For more than two years I had not written anything. Life was just passing by. I was in no way different from the millions trudging through life. Rather it was life which was dragging me along. Oh yes – I had a paycheck every month, a comfortable living standard - a perfect mediocre –

and a success in the eyes of most people. But was I living? I don't think so.

I was not doing the things I loved. I was in a situation I did not like at all. I hated the circumstances, which surrounded me. Getting up each morning was a labour. I was away from the things I loved.

That one instant when I smelt those flowers made me aware of what I was missing in life. I think I started turning around sometime during that period. My awareness had returned. The well known saying about 'smelling the flowers on the way' could not have been driven home to me in a more literal manner. As I turned the corner that day – I experienced - not merely understood the meaning of that saying.

It has driven home deeper lessons about the perils of compromising. One lands up having a life one does not really care to have. One ends up even deadening his own awareness. But then awareness is a powerful thing – at times it resurrects itself and gifts itself back to you.

One of the lessons learnt is – Beware!... or rather, Be Aware.

This was one of the smells, which made me feel it was good to be alive. But then something had gone wrong. I had stopped smelling these flowers.

*"Imperfection is beauty, madness is genius and it's better to be absolutely ridiculous than absolutely boring." – Marilyn Monroe*

# My Strength is my Weakness

My Self respect! I have been so proud of it. It made me what I am.

I never asked for favours because I was too proud to do so. As a student I never asked for money from my parents. I never asked my parents to send me on a school trip or vacation. I was respected in my circle of friends and acquaintances because I was considered to be an upright guy – with a lot of self esteem – one who would not give in to temptation easily.

I always thought of it as my strength.

But this strength was also my weakness as I was also too proud to run after girls. I was too proud to ask them for a date or a dance. The very thought of being turned down sent shivers through me. So I missed out on all those good times the boys of my age had.

At crucial junctures of my life, this trait came in my way. As a result I did not ask for that raise that I deserved. I did not insist on payment of the fees, which I had earned. I did not bargain hard enough in all those deals. I did not use that contact to pull that deal.... all because I was too proud to ask favours or too proud to ask for more money. In my mind I was always magnanimous even though I could not afford it.

So my pride also remained my weakness because it was not backed by the confidence that I needed. It does tell me that it is more of what I do with what I have that is important. Just having a trait is not enough by itself. It must be honed. Every aspect of one's character is a double-edged sword. The yin must follow the yang... and the yang must follow the yin.

It does make me think of my friend R__ who had tremendous dynamism. He repeatedly reached heights another person might take a lifetime to reach. The fire in his belly, which drove him was his strength. But that very fire landed him in trouble again and again. He kept leaving one city for the other. Until he found a balance...until the weakness and his strength brought him to an even keel.

Our strength makes us what we are, but if we cannot handle it, that very strength stops us from becoming what we can become.

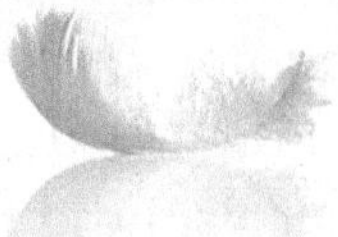

Just having a trait is not enough by itself. It must be honed. Every aspect of one's character is a double-edged sword. The yin must follow the yang… and the yang must follow the yin.

*"To thine own self be true, and it must follow, as the night the day, thou canst not then be false to any man." –William Shakespeare*

# That Boy!

Sometimes he wants to go out and play. At times he wants to walk in the rain. There are times he wants a midnight snack. At times he feels very naughty and wants to play pranks. He does manage to become a kid when he is with other kids. I see him getting tempted to do things he has not done in years. I know he would like to walk into people's homes at odd hours, just because he wants to chat. He feels like inviting himself to his friends' house for a meal or breakfast (and does so at times).

He is so spontaneous that I feel compelled to curb his spontaneity at times. He is so intense that he goes completely into relationships – and ends up getting hurt sometimes. That is why I want to protect him. Although somewhere deep down I know being protective will not help him – he must go through his share of pain. He is patient too. I know that he is waiting for the day when I can embrace him completely and merge with him.

For once upon a time I was him.

The 'I' that I had become was torn apart by so many demands that I had started keeping that boy away. But lately there has been a distinct change. He calls me more and more. I feel drawn to him more and more. Perhaps that is so because now I have started following myself. I know that within myself, there is a lot of sorting to be done yet. I know it is I, who has to take the steps. He will remain the faithful shadow. A shadow I had been trying to run away from.

I do not know how long it will take… for there are times when I feel that I am losing him. Times when he feels he is being deserted by his friends. That is when he goes to his corner and sulks. Those are the times when I harden. Then there are times when the world demands too much from me and I neglect him.

I am yet to resolve this. The day I can, I would cease to be a fragmented person. From that day, that boy and I would exist together as one ! And I shall guffaw again.

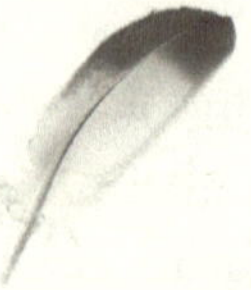

He is so intense that he goes completely into relationships – and ends up getting hurt sometimes. That is why I want to protect him. Although somewhere deep down I know being protective will not help him – he must go through his share of pain.

*"All the adversity I've had in my life, all my troubles and obstacles, have strengthened me... You may not realize it when it happens, but a kick in the teeth may be the best thing in the world for you". – Walt Disney*

# Are you looking for that Man?

You mean the man who did not have a fire in his belly? The one who had softness in him and who trusted blindly! You mean the guy who did not hit back and did not hit hard enough.

The man who did not have an ache in his heart?

Is it the same man whose gaze could not burn and whose tongue did not have enough acid? You mean the guy who was too polite to be frank. The same man who never learnt to emote.

Do you want the man who did not have enough guts to spell out his thoughts because they did not conform. Are you looking for the guy who was afraid to admit?

Are you looking for the man who did not pursue hard enough.

I am not sorry, but he does not live here anymore!

You mean the man who did not have a fire in his belly? The one who had softness in him and who trusted blindly! You mean the guy who did not hit back and did not hit hard enough.

*"Challenging the meaning of life is the truest expression of the state of being human."*
*– Viktor E. Frankl*

# That feeling of Emptiness – what is Needed to Fill it

When I feel alone I also feel empty. As I reach an age by which most men are supposed to have settled down I feel more unsettled than ever. The objectives of life seem clear and yet they seem farther than ever. At the same time they seem achievable because I feel I am now qualified to take on life. Battle scarred and weary at times, but confident nevertheless.

At yet another level I have also understood love in its various forms. In all its intriguing dimensions love has been accessible to me all my life. I have been touched by it – felt it – given it – and yet also felt its elusiveness.

Beauty and truth seem simple and so clear but the quest for both continues. It has been worth cherishing all that I have cherished. Why then do

I feel that there is a vacuum inside me? I am pretty sure that it is not caused by the hunger for more material success. Is it a yearning to prove myself in the eyes of the people who matter to me? Or is it the urge to establish the hunter in me?

Sometimes I feel it is because I am yet to do something special with my life. A purpose I have not yet found or fulfilled but am inching towards.

One thing is for certain... whatever is needed to fill this emptiness will come to me when I am ready for it – when I deserve it.

Why then do I feel that there is a vacuum inside me? I am pretty sure that it is not caused by the hunger for more material success. Is it a yearning to prove myself in the eyes of the people who matter to me? Or is it the urge to establish the hunter in me?

*"A loving heart is the beginning of all knowledge."– Thomas Carlyle*

# Reaching Out

How easy it is, to go on living like animals. Perhaps millions of us do it - eating, sleeping, mating & fearing. Never really trying go beyond this. Oh yes always doing what the society expects us to keep doing - going to work, raising a family, socializing. But always living at the periphery – never really making a difference anywhere. Perhaps a large chunk of my life I also lived like that. It was nothing more than the life of a zombie.

Completely deaf!

Completely blind!

Devoid of the sensitivity that makes us human.

Otherwise how could I have failed to perceive the pain that some of my friends were going through.

Two of them almost committed suicide!

And I was not even aware.

Most of the time I was going through life without feeling anything! Like anyone else I had taken shelter under the typical behaviour we have learned to adopt – when faced with unpleasant truths or situations which require effort from your side, just avoid or postpone the situation - hoping that the problems or situations would just go away. Not saying something unpleasant because it may affect your popularity. Not getting involved. Busy with our own rut. The rut we try to pretend is so important, lying to ourselves, day in and day out... shutting out our awareness and sensitivity.

Should I have waited for a friend to ask for help or should I have reached out when I felt it was important to do so. Could I have made a difference in their lives? I do think so. My presence would have certainly have given them strength. I think I failed them at a crucial juncture of their lives.

One thing is for sure my involvement would certainly have made a difference in my own life. It would have made a difference in the way I perceived myself. But I chose to live like any other zombie – all hunky-dory from the 'normal' standards, but miserably failing my own as I see them.

I can never make up for what I did not do but the least I can do is wake up now and make sure that I reach out before a crisis strikes.

I suppose there can be no growth unless I set out to achieve tougher standards set out by my own self.

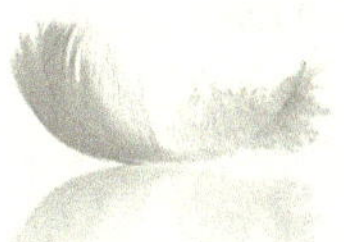

But I chose to live like any other zombie – all hunky-dory from the 'normal' standards, but miserably failing my own as I see them.

*"You are always free to change your mind and choose a different future, or a different past."*
*–Richard Bach*

# The Real World

My anger, desire or love, do not exist outside of me. They have no place in the world of objects and things. And yet these are the ultimate subjective reality for me- very real, very concrete – and the most important reality in the world. Whatever I have felt deeply, is the only truth I know. It is only that, which has remained with me – is a part of me. In the ultimate analysis, I suppose, this is what life means. Whatever I have not felt has not really happened for me! Life, to me, is nothing but this ability to feel.

It leads me to an inescapable conclusion that each one of us lives in a different world. Whatever we feel and desire remains our single most important drive of life. Anything that happens – no matter when or where, gets life only because we feel it and make it a part of us. Otherwise it is lost forever. As good as it never happened.

Our feelings make us – drive us – propel us – and are responsible for all that happens to us. The 'practical' people of the world have always had the tendency to refer to these realities as 'merely psychological'. As if psychological was not real!

Most positive attitudinal lessons that are given to us are dismissed by pessimists as so many tricks to console ourselves; little realising that attitudes are about transformation and there is nothing more real than transformation. Consolation is from the outside & transformation is from within. Perhaps, if we are to really understand our own existence in this world we need to understand this most important aspect of our existence, away from the philosophizing. Our feelings are the most concrete part of our reality... the most important reality... the reality which is completely our own.

Yes, we do share a common physical world. But this is only a small part of reality where our individual world overlaps with the worlds of other beings. Each of us exists very much within the ambit of feelings, desires and emotions. These feelings and desires have not only propelled my life – they would perhaps carry me into another dimension beyond these external world that I have perceived all along – and take me into a world where I would exist as nothing but the personification of these feelings.

Will this central aspect of life take me onto another life? A life where I would need to live out all that I have sought hitherto – the love, longing, riches, hatreds, achievements, frustrations – all the hankering which has gone into shaping this life.

Is that what life is all about? Seeking fulfillment of our deepest desires and feelings across the vast reaches of space and time!

The 'practical' people of the world have always had the tendency to refer to these realities as 'merely psychological'. As if psychological was not real!

*"There are more things in heaven and earth, Horatio, than are dreamt of in your philosophy". – Hamlet by William Shakespeare*

# Call from the other side...

In the early nineties, one hot summer afternoon when I was in Rajasthan busy with some plantation work, we had to go from Ratangarh to Muamasar a remote village in Rajasthan to meet someone. I was quite familiar with this unique and beautiful land with its simple people. But, it was the first time that I had stayed in Rajasthan for some length of time as an adult. The enchanting land always held a special charm for me. To me this was a land where you could touch history.... could feel the bygone era.... could see the customs being followed in its unadulterated form for centuries....

Since this was the time of sandstorms and high temperatures, we started in the late afternoon to avoid the scorching heat. After turning off from the Highway we were on to a one lane road. Once on it, we drove for miles without sighting any settlements. The craggy and misshapen trees with a scattering of some bushes and the sand dunes here and there were the only features you could see. Yet the land had a strange beauty. Sandstorms were common phenomena during these summer months and wherever the road went up an incline there were substantial sand deposits on the road making passage a little difficult. We got stuck in the sand on one such hillock and managed to get out with some difficulty. While the rest of the journey was uneventful I was struck by the fact that the area was unusually desolate even by Rajasthan standards. We had our meeting at Muamasar and by the time we started back after having a wonderful dinner, it was midnight.

The town was dimly lit & desolate and we did not see even a stray dog as we drove out. After a drive of about half an hour we reached the hillock we had got stuck on. We stopped the jeep just before the crest of the hillock and two of us got down to ensure that the path that the jeep took was not over the soft sand to avoid getting stuck again. As I felt the sand with my foot the driver reversed the jeep so as to come back with sufficient speed & momentum to cross the sand deposit on the road. Once I had made sure of the path to be taken I pointed it out and beckoned to the jeep driver. "Aa jao" I called out.

A second later I heard someone else call out the same thing.

"Aa jao…aa jao" (Come over…come over)

I heard it clearly. I looked to my left down the small hillock. Even in the moonlight the visibility was pretty good. The hair on the nape of my neck bristled. The desert-air was cool but not cold enough to give me goose pimples. But the sound of those innocuous words did. As I stood there beside the road in the middle of a barren landscape from my high vantage point I could see that there was no one for miles around. And yet I heard the voice clearly. I scanned the area yet again and in the clear moonlight I could see that there was virtually no cover for anyone.

A few small thorny bushes were scattered around but not even a dog could have hidden in them. There was no way any human being could be hiding anywhere within hundreds of yards.

A small red light glowed in the direction of the voice and then faded as if someone had taken a drag of a 'beedi'. But there was no one there. The light hung in mid air and then disappeared. Was it a firefly? But fireflies emit a green light! There was something very strange happening here!! The red glow came on again and faded slowly.

"Aa jao…aa jao" (Come over…come over)… I heard the eerie voice again. I looked around carefully. There was no one. The call was repeated a third time. "Did you hear that" I asked my companion across the road. He was silent…. I took the hint and went quiet. A moment later the jeep came over and crossed the difficult spot. We quickly hopped in and drove off.

While the jeep sped through the darkness we sat in silence, quite shaken. For a long time neither of us spoke. We were a little numb after this very strange encounter. "You should not have spoken" was all that my companion had to say. The folk lore in Rajasthan is that if you hear some strange voice in the night you do not answer… for it is a call from the other side. When you answer you may just open a door for some unwanted presence in your life.

I am certain about one thing…. There was no human being out there for there was nowhere to hide. It was the middle of nowhere in the middle of the night. No human being had any reason to be out there let alone call out to us in that fashion.

Was it indeed a "Call from the other Side?"

I could see that there was no one for miles around. And yet I heard the voice clearly. I scanned the area yet again and in the clear moonlight I could see that there was virtually no cover for anyone.

*"Quantum theory also tells us that the world is not simply objective; somehow it's something more subtle than that. In some sense it is veiled from us, but it has a structure that we can understand." – John Polkinghorne*

# The Subtle Patterns of Life

Is our happiness related to the places we live in or with the people who are around us in some way or the other?

Not in the sense that it does not flow from outside but perhaps in a deeper way. Perhaps in the sense that we need to seek out and live out our destiny in a certain time & place... perhaps in the sense that the fulfillment of what we seek in life, is deeply entwined with a place or a particular environment. There are places, which seem intertwined with your destiny. There are people who seem to have an inescapable part in your happiness. Inevitably, you only seem to find happiness when you are in those places.

Happiness seems to find you when you are with those people or you find yourself sharing your best moments and achievements with them – celebrating with them. Good times seem to elude you when you are away from those people or places.

It is true that the happiness or the best times of our lives are not flowing to us from these places or people but certainly they are playing a key part in this flow, taking place. Is that why we are drawn to such places and people? In a way and partly, this linkage has come to be known as destiny.

There are places, which seem intertwined with your destiny. There are people who seem to have an inescapable part in your happiness. Inevitably, you only seem to find happiness when you are in those places.

*"Blessed are they who see beautiful things in humble places where other people see nothing." – Camille Pissarro*

# Just Look Sideways

I found another world out there. A different world from the one I had been seeing.

It was very much a physical world – a world of people and houses. And yet, it was so very different.

For years, I had traveled on the road looking straight ahead, never really bothering to turn my head. But one day I looked to one side. And I saw a world, which was so different from the one I had been so used to seeing. I saw a world of by lanes & alleys. I saw a world of corridors & side entrances. I saw a world of ducts and pipes – a world of quaint houses and forgotten architecture.

I saw a world of partially hidden houses which could only be glimpsed from the street. It was also a world of dead-end lanes and squalor. It was a world frozen in time. Sometimes I saw it as the refuge of the unwanted. And sometimes it revealed itself as an oasis of beauty & grace, within a locality of chaos.

I fell in love with this world. Whenever I can, I still look sideways. I have always managed to find a city within a city, a town within a town and a village within a village. Ugly or beautiful, quaint or simple, attractive or repulsive – no matter what, this world is fascinating.

The hidden courtyards, the crumbling staircases, the hutment behind the houses, the neat lanes and the dumping grounds, the leaking pipes and the diffident people – they are all invisible until I turn my head.

In the ultimate analysis, this is all it takes, a slight turn of the head – and you find new worlds & new dimensions.

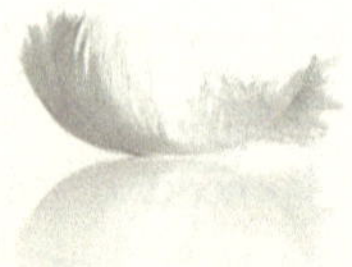

I saw a world of by lanes & alleys. I saw a world of corridors & side entrances. I saw a world of ducts and pipes – a world of quaint houses and forgotten architecture.

*"The most important kind of freedom is to be what you really are. You trade in your reality for a role. You give up your ability to feel, and in exchange, put on a mask." – Jim Morrison*

# We Hide Ourselves from others in so Many Ways

Why are we afraid to tell others who we are?

We take tremendous pain to don carefully crafted masks, always trying to hide behind them. Very carefully we play the father, mother, employee or professional, never letting the mask slip; so much so that we forget to take off these masks even when we are alone. We start playing a character – even believing in that character. We manage to lose ourselves completely. Look around you and you will see what I mean.

See the stiff upper lip. See the stifled laughter. Hear the suppressed sneeze.

You sit stiffly when you want to sing and dance. He shakes hands when he wants to embrace. I choose to project the picture of dignity when I really want to jump with joy. Always trying to be what we believe we ought to be like and in the process destroying what we essentially are. Why is it so difficult to wear my heart on my sleeve?

We have become a race of scared people – so insecure and unsure of ourselves. As if we are scared of being eaten up if we dare to reveal ourselves, living in our own cocoons; feeling too vulnerable to reveal our true self. But then what is the point if we are too scared to be ourselves. It takes strength to reveal your true self. It takes confidence and self-assuredness to be able to do that. But we have been brought up to believe otherwise. The result is sad. We are not loved for who we really are. The person we project is the one that is loved (or admired or envied for that matter). And whenever we do reveal ourselves we are rejected.... by the very persons whom we have deceived over the years.

But the tragedy goes even deeper than this. Over the years we lose ourselves. Since we have been unable to accept ourselves, we fail to express ourselves. We live the lives of fictitious characters, and die unfulfilled.

Nothing but a life wasted!

The result is sad.
We are not loved for who we really are. The person we project is the one that is loved (or admired or envied for that matter). And whenever we do reveal ourselves we are rejected.... by the very persons whom we have deceived over the years.

*"Laughter is the shortest distance between two people." – Yakov Smirnoff*

# Laughter

When I am not, GOD is! When the ego is takes leave, GOD happens! People lose themselves in the frenzy of dance. Some experience HIM in the cessation of thoughts in the deepest realms of meditation. Yet others get a glimpse of him as they are immersed in music. ME! The closest that I come to lose the sense of everything is when I laugh & make others laugh. Nothing else exists then, it is just me and the laughter. I always feel then, that there can be no greater purpose to existence than a heartfelt laughter. It is therapy; it is explosion of joy; it is a lifetime fitted into a few seconds; it is love of life; it is a fountain which springs from life.

It has beauty; it has depth; it has the understanding of eons; it has the stillness of existence; it has the flash of revelation; it has the blessings of the Gods; it has the scorn of the devil.

Above all it is the kiss of life, it is the only thing Man spreads selflessly towards all – even love does not reach as far and as impartially as laughter. Spreading a joke is the greatest act of compassion that a man can commit.

And yes, I have had the fortune of being close to someone who lives for laughter, who epitomizes laughter.... someone for whom, every moment is a moment for laughter, someone whose sense of humour will not abandon him even when he is breathing his last. A___, has been the greatest inspiration as well as a catalyst for laughter in my life. I find my own sense of humour responding to the laughter energy that he carries around with him. Whenever we meet it is laugh riot. It rarely happens with anyone else. Perhaps the reason is that he is a clean soul who he is not afraid of laying himself bare. There are no pretensions, no masks and therefore the fountain of laughter just flows. In some way, whenever he is around, this energy & purity touches my core and I respond from deep within – honestly and without inhibition – for laughter is one of the purest human emotions. I am blessed that I had people like him around me to show that the meaning of life need not be anything more than a good laugh.

I laugh. I enjoy the company of people who create laughter. I love making people laugh. What else is there to discuss! The discourse is over!

ME! The closest that I come to lose the sense of everything is when I laugh & make others laugh. Nothing else exists then, it is just me and the laughter. I always feel then, that there can be no greater purpose to existence than a heartfelt laughter.

*"For the wise man looks into space and he knows there are no limited dimensions."*
*–Lao Tzu*

## I Belong to the Stars

There is something magical about the night sky! Deep & mysterious it is, no doubt. But there is something more to it. The vastness is scary but there is a pull also – pull of a different planet. A pull so strong that it lingers long after the magic of the night has disappeared in to the daylight. A pull so strong it makes me feel that there is more than a single home for us. Earth is so familiar and comforting. And yet this pull of a far away planet has stayed across so many years. Have I lived somewhere else also in this vastness?

The physical vastness of this universe is overpowering and makes me feel insignificant and yet in another way my spirit soars. In another way strangely enough, the night sky somehow makes me aware of my own vastness.

Something inside tells me I have been out there somewhere. My consciousness does not accept any limitations. It tells me it has been in other places in that vast myriad of light specks. It tells me, I am neither body bound nor earth bound. This longing convinces me that I am indeed a spiritual being, a being which can choose his home anywhere. There are other homes which await this boundless spirit.

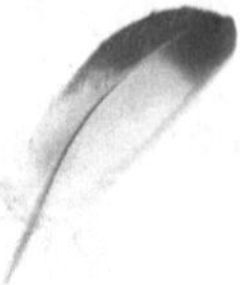

The physical vastness of this universe is overpowering and makes me feel insignificant and yet in another way my spirit soars. In another way strangely enough, the night sky somehow makes me aware of my own vastness.

*"Your sacred space is where you can find yourself again and again." – Joseph Campbell*

# That Sacred Corner Inside

I stood in front of the Haveli (*old fashioned private mansion*). I had come after years! It still looked quite similar, only a lot smaller. *(the childhood memories were of a much larger structure… I suppose I had grown and as a consequence the Haveli had shrunk)* This is where I had spent a part of my early childhood. The house held a lot of childhood memories. I could visualize the steep stone staircase which was so intimidating to me as a child; the stepping stone which made a distinct sound as you stepped on it to enter the 'aangan' (atrium); the small barred windows and the terrace which always had a few monkeys loitering around at any given time.

A part of the sprawling house still belonged to a cousin. But the major part had been sold off. But I know the innards had changed. People had spoilt the look - using grills to create separate demarcated portions to live in. Some strangers were living there.

What it looks like now would destroy some part of my memory – would defile a sacred space inside me.

No, I would not go inside!

What it looks like now would destroy some part of my memory – would defile a sacred space inside me.

*"But man is not made for defeat. A man can be destroyed but not defeated."*
*– Ernest Hemingway*

# Defeat

Without defeat there can be no hunger – there can be no fire, the intense burning that scalds your insides and does not let you sleep till you succeed. Until you have been defeated you cannot become an achiever. So whenever you are defeated know that you are blessed for you are now going to grow, you are ready to receive – you are eligible to receive.

Habitual winners are not getting ready for what matters in life - they will not invest enough in themselves and therefore cannot become as enriched as a person who has faced defeat in life.

When you face defeat with awareness, you can understand what defeat wanted to teach you... you do not miss the lesson. It is then you realize that it was the lesson which was the purpose not the defeat. The defeat only accompanied the lesson to ensure that you learnt.

I am thankful to every defeat in my life for all that was worthwhile in my life was taught to me by defeat – losing money while speculating; losing my temper and facing the consequences; befriending the wrong kind of persons and paying the price; putting money into grandiose schemes and losing it… all the important lessons came when I apparently lost. But I thank God for those defeats… because those very defeats shaped me by driving home the 'value' lessons that I needed.

And if you have truly faced defeat, it only remains an event in your life - an event that you outgrow. You realize then that defeat was never a problem… accepting any defeat as final was the problem. You realize then, that YOU can never be defeated.

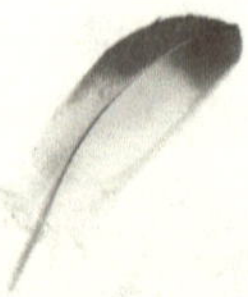

So whenever you are defeated know that you are blessed for you are now going to grow, you are ready to receive – you are eligible to receive.

*"What I spent, I had. What I kept, I lost. But what I gave, I HAVE."*

## Let go...

Why has love come to mean just holding on? Just trying to be together is certainly not love! But in the name of love I see people just holding on to their 'loved' ones, whether it is wife, husband, children or girlfriend. And the irony is that this holding on is what leads to the death of love. Holding on, can only be the resultant effect of fear, certainly not love. If someone were to hold on to me, the first thing that would die would be the love I felt for that person.

In fact it holds good for all that is valuable in life. Whenever we try to hold on to anything that is precious to us, be it happiness, peace or love we lose it for sure.

But I suppose, most of us make this mistake because we have been brought up with the 'tangible' mind set and we have always thought that like tangible things the best way to keep a good thing going is to keep it under lock & key. Love is a state of being, a state of doing not having or owning. It is the most valuable thing in life and it is always there - readily available, easily accessible, always flowing - all we need to do is to give of it as much as we can.

Perhaps the most intense and natural love that we feel is for our offspring. But so often, I have found people holding on to their children even after they have grown up. Their stranglehold never allows them to set up their own home. If my daughter is to have a loving home it has to be one which is inspired by the love she saw in our home and not one which is directed by my ever present shadow. Some of the divorces which need never have happened were where one spouse wanted a release – not from the partner but from his / her 'concerned' parent. Such parents could never let go and it was the desire to own their child, which destroyed any possibility of the child blooming into a loving individual. But the tragedy is that such love suffocates and kills the spirit for it is no love – it is merely a desire to hold on, a desire to possess. The giving is missing from such 'love' that is what makes it poisonous. I have seen some of such parents succeed in holding on to their children – I also see the everlasting misery that they managed to create for their children and themselves.

And then there are parents who make their children so loving and who are so generous with their love that they ensure that their children set up homes which are as loving as the ones they themselves had created. Such parents know that they are merely fulfilling a cycle. They themselves could create a loving home because of their own parents who could love and then let go.

To use a cliché, it happens because such people know the secret of love - give it away and a lot more of it will come back to you; set the ones you love free and they will be yours forever.

Until I let go the world will not get an additional loving home. Only, in my letting go... love multiplies!!

Whenever we try to hold on to anything that is precious to us, be it happiness, peace or love we lose it for sure.

*"What we have once enjoyed we can never lose.All that we love deeply becomes a part of us."*
*– Helen Keller*

# Owning by Assent

I own all that is beautiful and all that I love. I own it not in the physical sense but at a much deeper level. Whenever, I have seen lovely works of creation, beautiful paintings, profound pieces of writing… some part of me reached out to embrace these things. In that moment I felt I owned that thing. These things would always be a part of me kept in the depths of my being where I can dive in and appreciate and caress them whenever I want.

Whether it is God's creation or man's, matters little, for all creation is divine and so is the love I feel for all that I respond favorably to. I own that lovely green valley, that lovely villa by the sea; that fantastic painting; that melodious ghazal and that bonsai plant for I have given my assent to them. They have come to me unconditionally in a dimension, which is solely, mine. That unbridled laughter of that small child, the wistful look on that elderly gentleman's face and that smile on that beautiful woman's face - they are as much mine as they are of the person's who display them.

That is why perhaps the more you contribute in the lives of others, the richer you become; the more you appreciate the good things in life without jealousy or envy; the more easily and truly do you own them. The presence of any negative feeling means that I have denied access to that thing of beauty and so naturally, it cannot give me joy even for a moment, let alone forever.

These things would always be a part of me kept in the depths of my being where I can dive in and appreciate and caress them whenever I want.

*"Help others achieve their dreams and you will achieve yours." – Les Brown*

# My Circle of Influence

"How should I deal with hurt? How do I convince a person I love that his actions are causing me hurt. What if he does not even understand or acknowledge the hurt he is causing? "

So many times such questions crop up in some form or the other reflecting the internalized hurts of a person. More often than not, this hurt is carried by women and sensitive men. And more often than not, they seek answers outside, trying to change the people who matter in their lives. But is it possible for anyone to change another? The answer could be YES and NO. It is NO in the sense that no one really has the power to change another person. That is why the attempts, though genuine fail.

And yet you have a certain other power. The power to empower... You can empower another person to change himself, motivate him enough to grow. But what kind of a person can really empower another or how does one acquire this power of empowerment! Certainly if I do not have the power over myself I cannot be in a position to empower another. One has to start at a very basic level. My own experience tells me that one acquires this power when you have no wish to have any power over others. Only when I am totally rooted in some deeply held principles and convictions do I really become powerful. This is really a journey towards fearlessness. Only a fearless person can have power. Because it is only then that his wish to dominate someone else goes. The fearful of this world are always trying to dominate others. They are desperate and scared and they do so lest they be dominated. It is a defense mechanism.

Once I start growing stronger my power of empowerment goes up. In my own life I found that without knowing it, I started influencing people only when I got rooted in certain principles, only when I became a stronger person myself; only when I was acting out of love and without any selfish motives. With this went up the strength to deal with any hurt as well. You do really learn to change what you can, bear with what you cannot and also perhaps get the wisdom to know the difference.

At the same time I must accept that since life is dynamic the relationships cannot be static! Is it not a fallacy to expect them to remain so? My relationship with my wife, my friends, acquaintances, relatives, professional colleagues has always been in a state of flux. As I look back as I see clearly that we either grew together or grew apart. Physically you may be together with anyone but that is only one realm of reality. If mentally, intellectually and spiritually I start drifting away from someone the real separation has begun. Once this reality of life is accepted, my helplessness towards relationships ceases – I do not try to change what cannot be changed.

I do know this journey of growth and self-discovery is not easy. But it is worth all the hurt that may have come along the way. Pain, I suppose is a part of life, but how much I suffer is largely a matter of choice. My strength can go up only when I can take the pain that life has thrown my way. Until I have enough strength I cannot hope to empower anyone!

Once I have found myself at this deeper level, the answer as to how to deal with the pain and the hurt will come on its own. It cannot really come from anyone else. My circle of influence will be in tune with what I am. The stronger & deeper I am.... the less I wish for power over others... the bigger would be my circle of influence.... the more power to empower I shall have...

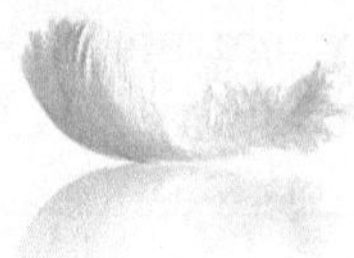

And yet you have a certain other power. The power to empower... You can empower another person to change himself, motivate him enough to grow.

*The more we live guided from within,*
*the greater our control over outer events*
*in the great game of life.*
*For when we live at our own center,*
*in super consciousness,*
*we live in the only true freedom there is.*
*Omar Khayyam's Rubaiyat (Stanza fifty)*

# Living by Principles

Life principles cannot be derived from utopian theories. These principles are time tested and universal. Principles like Justice, Fair play, Honesty, Liberty. The principles are the ones, which stand the test of non-malice and balanced living. These principles are accepted by everyone but not practiced on the grounds of impracticality.

My life did not work for me whenever I deviated from the basic principles of life.

At times, sticking by the principles seemed stupid. But as I look back I see that whatever I cherish is with me because I stuck to the principles – as opposed to narrow definitions of morality and "dos and don'ts". In the ultimate analysis I can see that my friends still love me for what I basically am and not by the worldly success I have had. Of course what I achieve in life is a way of telling people what I am. The degree of public recognition or success as it is known may vary.

Today I can say with conviction that no matter what may appear to the world, a man knows that whenever he gets something by compromising with principles it never gets him happiness although it may get him a fat bank balance for some time. But everything goes the way it comes. Otherwise it pushes out from our lives all that which is far more precious. Of course most of us do not have the wisdom to understand the link between what we gain by that compromise and what we lose.

Utopian theories seem to fill people with a sense of self-righteousness – the feeling that all else is wrong and no price is too small to pay for that utopia. Such theories do not have compassion as their foundation and as a result only end up bringing misery. As opposed to that, Principles are there for you to practice and not for imposing on others. The basis of Principles is always compassion. That is why they have stood the test of time.

By sticking to the principles we believe in, we simply stick to what we are and we become more of what we can become. By deviating from principles we always get fragmented. We tend to give away what we are so that we may become something we are not. We start living the life of someone else, someone who would be perceived as successful – not someone who has achieved something – not someone who has done something worthwhile.

Principles would always lead us to achievement. They allow us to blossom, for living a life of principles means living in harmony, living naturally, living for the right things. I think I started discovering myself only when I stopped compromising with principles. The surprising thing was that I found it much easier, for it came as naturally as breathing.

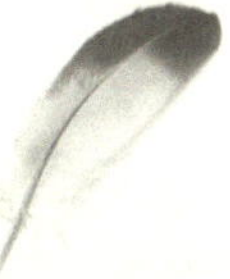

By deviating from principles we always get fragmented. We tend to give away what we are so that we may become something we are not. We start living the life of someone else, someone who would be perceived as successful – not someone who has achieved something – not someone who has done something worthwhile.

*"The best and most beautiful things in the world cannot be seen or even touched. They must be felt within the heart."*
*– Helen Keller*

# Daughter Again...

I woke up with a start. It had been an uneasy night, since my younger daughter had had a sun stroke the previous day. As a result she was running a high temperature and was suffering from diarrhea. Dehydration was very much there so I was administering a regular dosage of ORS to her. As a two year old she was suffering silently and compounding my feeling of guilt because I had taken her up to the terrace of our ancestral house in Mathura for taking some photographs in searing heat.

The reason why it was so important for me was that I wanted my children to feel and be a part of my own childhood. I wanted them to connect with my roots. This paternal home was the place where I instantly relived my childhood the moment I reached there. Every nook & corner of the huge house held a memory. In my eagerness to have maximum photographs possible, we spent far too long in the fierce sun and within a few hours she was ill.

Now, as I woke up I found my face was inches away from her rear.  Before I could move she defecated on my face. I hardly flinched. After I had cleaned up I was amazed at myself. What makes a father so very naturally accept, everything that his child does. Life keeps teaching you the meaning of love. Loving your child can be so different from loving your parent. And yet there is an undercurrent which is the same. The intensity of this love flows in torrents towards your children.

My younger daughter took her own time to learn to talk (and to walk for that matter). But when she eventually did there was no stopping her. Throughout her childhood (and even today) she always came to me whenever we stepped out of the house. As a result she always managed to soil my clothes. Be it vomiting on me during a drive up the hills or be it urinating in the bed as an infant, in her time of discomfort she would always seek me out and manage to find relief in whatever way she could.

The strange thing was that in my love for her I could find another aspect of being a parent. I had been more of a father all along but slowly and surely I had now become a little bit of a mother as well.

Even today when she is emotionally disturbed I know that she will respond to me. She knows that she will reach out to me. I also know that she will come to me. This trust managed to soften the rebellious streak that existed in her. I suppose the need to rebel dissolves if a child knows that a parent is willing to listen and understand. It also enables the child to take a verbal lashing or a disciplinary action against her in the right spirit. She could always see my love in the harshness that sometimes I had to mete out. I think she never doubted my love for her and that enabled her to overcome her doubts about my actions.

This is the bond that any parent would want – that your child understands that you are there for her when she needs you. And you know that she will seek you when it matters. If such moments are missed the whole purpose of parenting is missed. God made parents only for this purpose. Our purpose, as parents is met when we are just there ........ .

Life keeps teaching you the meaning of love. Loving your child can be so different from loving your parent. And yet there is an undercurrent which is the same. The intensity of this love flows in torrents towards your children.

*"In the realm of ideas everything depends on enthusiasm... in the real world all rests on perseverance."*
*– Johann Wolfgang von Goethe*

# Hopes & Ideas

Let us not hope in the manner of people who put their eggs in the fridge and hope to get a whole lot of chicken streaming out of it one fine morning. Seeds of ideas, wishes and hopes need the warmth of spontaneity, daring and action before they can start germinating. I cannot count the number of ideas I have lost because I did not keep them warm this way.

Whether it was a business idea or the idea of a party or an idea of a piece of writing, or just the wish of an unusual outing, they have all been lost because I never warmed up to them, never dared to do something about them. What do I have to blame for it? My own curbing of my spontaneity has been one of the causes.

I do not remember the ideas themselves, but I do remember I had quite a few ideas for pieces of writing. But I simply failed to capture them.

There is still that wish for the trek in that forest. I still hope to live a life of romance. But what am I doing for it?

But now I am determined not to lose these divine gifts. I keep a diary for my ideas and dreams. The day I got the first thoughts, which appear in this book, I sat on the computer and started hammering the keyboard. Before I could realise it, concrete shape of things to come was emerging. For too long I had put my spontaneity away, now I shall live with it. For me, that is going to be the way to savour life from now on. And it is already beginning to take effect. Some more daring, some more spontaneity that is what I need! I need to be much more alert.

Aey mere dil, thoda aur deewana ban yaar!

[Put in a dash of madness in your life man!]

Seeds of ideas, wishes and hopes need the warmth of spontaneity, daring and action before they can start germinating. I cannot count the number of ideas I have lost because I did not keep them warm this way.

*"By giving people the power to share, we're making the world more transparent."*
*- Mark Zuckerberg*

# Something More the Internet has Done

Although Internet has been appreciated all over the world for opening up communication in physical terms, to my mind, one of the most beautiful things the net has done is that it has enabled individuals to open up in so many ways. The pros & cons may be argued for whatever they are worth but the fact remains that while communicating to others through the net, individuals are diving deeper into themselves. In the process of talking to others they are getting in touch with their own dreams, desires and wishes.

When I write on the computer and communicate with another person I may or may not know, I lay bare my innermost thoughts, ideas and feelings. It is as if each and every thought is surgically cut open - its intestines showing. The innermost reaches of my mind are exposed to another person for the first time. Thoughts which you may not have had an occasion to share, wishes you could not share, desires which you thought may be unacceptable to the people around you, fantasies you thought would shock the love in your life - all these and so much more comes pouring out.

Not only do you communicate, you also get in touch with the innermost core of yourself. The beginnings of understanding yourself may also lie here.

Perhaps this happens because it is such a secure world. There is no need for you to guard yourself, no need for you to project yourself, no need for you to hide your thoughts and ideas lest anyone may laugh at you. For me the sheer joy of diving into myself and finding someone who may share his own innermost recesses of his/her mind is so beautiful and stimulating. Ideally, we should also be doing this with the persons we love in our own life, but then we need to seek so many dimensions of our own being and this is the easiest and the most effective way the Net has opened up for us.

Thoughts which you may not have had an occasion to share, wishes you could not share, desires which you thought may be unacceptable to the people around you, fantasies you thought would shock the love in your life - all these and so much more comes pouring out.

*"An intellectual is a person who's found one thing that's more interesting than sex."*
*– Aldous Huxley*

# Sex – The Complete Union

The word 'sex' arouses so many reactions and emotions including those ranging from complete disgust to complete rapture. One reaction cannot stand the other. People react to sex quite strongly. Men and women approach it so very differently in spite of needing each other to do it. There is a tussle in the very approach to sex. Because of this, women tend to feel men are totally different creatures. To them the attitude of men is totally inexplicable. Men in turn perceive a total indifference in women towards sex. Both read each other so very wrongly.

No matter what the tussle may be, fact remains that sex is the most natural thing on earth. Our entire planet is engaged in sex - it is perhaps the most frequently indulged in activity. If we recognise that we are essentially multi dimensional creatures the approach to sex can be understood a little better and perhaps the two sexes will not be so foxed by each other's behaviour and approach towards sex.

Sex is the need of a human being to deeply and intimately connect with another person on the physical plane. Of course the approach to sex may be made from either mental / intellectual or the biological plane. For some people coupling on the physical plane alone is sex. Then there are others who would not get into bed with anyone without feeling any emotions for the person. Those who are more rooted in their intellect need to relate on this plane and can have a lasting relationship only if this happens. The approach may be from any of the planes but the manifestation is on the physical plane.

Men are believed to be physical - ever ready to jump into bed with a desirable woman at the drop of a hat – it maybe so. But I for one feel that truly satisfying sex can happen only when a man and a woman relate on almost all the planes. One can approach an erotic relationship from the physical dimension alone - it can be explosive but chances are that lasting and deeply satisfying sex would not be there, in spite of the intensity that one may feel and the relationship may prove to be effervescent. When a man who is balanced in all the dimensions of his existence, seeks to connect, he wants to connect on all levels and dimensions. When he tends to reach out and have sex he is likely to do so with someone he can relate with on most levels and dimensions. He does not seek something frivolous.

And yet the paradox is that he does not cease to be a primal creature deep inside. There are times and moments in his life when he is purely driven by his physical urge - to couple with a woman who arouses his lust. That is why his behaviour at times may seem contradictory. But most often than not such balanced men are able to keep this urge under control and let go only in exceptional circumstances.

Women find this weakness inexplicable. For their basic need lies in the realm of feelings. Only when this need is fulfilled does she open herself to sex. Her need for sex is only stimulated once the primary need for feeling cherished is satisfied. Sex only seems to be a corollary.

Thus I see men who stay in the physical dimension and have sex all the time without really reaching out. Since they cease to connect on the other planes they never really learn how to make love. As a result theirs is a very frustrating chase because what they seek continues to elude them. The emptiness they feel is because what they are doing is just one-dimensional.

Obviously, you cannot put sex in a slot *per se.* It is the intent and purpose behind sex that really decides its characteristic. When someone pays for it - it is release, when it is forced - it is rape, when done for the heck of it - it is habit. The real dimension lies in the brain - the physical act in stark terms is almost the same. One act can bring ecstasy and another abhorrence.

When you approach sex through the mental dimension, the maturity level and depth is of course far greater. When you have sex with someone with whom you connect at all levels you can experience ecstasy; because in the ultimate analysis sex is the urge to seek union and union in just one dimension can never match the complete union which encompasses all levels.

In this union, men and women essentially seek partners who complement them. Their masculinity and feminity must fulfill each other, THAT is when they achieve a remarkable fulfillment. Otherwise a feeling of emptiness or a sense of loss is bound to remain.

The union through sex can be complete only if we learn to relate at more and deeper levels.

When a man who is balanced in all the dimensions of his existence, seeks to connect, he wants to connect on all levels and dimensions. When he tends to reach out and have sex he is likely to do so with someone he can relate with on most levels and dimensions. He does not seek something frivolous.

*"We are not human beings having a spiritual experience. We are spiritual beings having a human experience."*
*– Pierre Teilhard de Chardin*

# It is Written...

"You are the only son in your family. Your father's name is......; your mother is no more, her name was....; your wife's name is......; your name is Abhay, you are in consultancy line, you were born on ....; presently you are .... years old; you were born under... Rashi and ... Nakshatra; you have two daughters, the elder one has finished her studies and is doing a job, younger daughter is doing something that is technical & artistic at the same time..........."

The man was rattling off my personal facts in ancient Tamil from an obviously very old 'patra' which had been located from a mass of such 'patras' on the basis of my thumb print! There was no way he could have known any of these facts about me. As the translator narrated all this I could only listen dumbfounded! How was it possible? How could such facts about me have been recorded in an ancient text? How could my situation in life at the time of my visit also been foretold? As people nowadays are very found of saying 'How could I swallow all this in this age of science & technology?' (*The fact that these people have no clue about the science & technology that they swear by is another matter!*)

My interest in the para-normal sciences was very old. Intuitively I believed that there was substance in these things – the tricksters & charlatans notwithstanding. After all the existence of quacks does not disprove medical science – does it? I had spent years researching these subjects, but I always on the look out for concrete personal experiences which would establish this belief into an unshakeable knowledge. Over the years, I visited a number of astrologers, more to understand the knowledge & wisdom behind this ancient science than to know my own future. But never had I come across such irrefutable proof of this miraculous 'Vidya' (*knowledge*).

My future was seen and written by someone thousands of years ago!!!...not only my future but also timing of my visit to the centre of 'Naadi Jyotish' was foreseen. If I had had my 'patra' read a few months before, the reading would not be correct as my daughter would still be studying and not working!

An ancient sage – Agastya, foresaw the future of thousands of persons and wrote about each one in amazing detail. Interestingly, the foretelling also involved laying down penances for the wrong deeds done over previous births & offering an alternate destiny on a path chosen by the soul in that birth.

The fact that it foretold all the milestones of this birth, although astounding, is not the REAL revelation. The miracle or the transformational revelation was twofold. In one stroke two things happened. Firstly, what was merely an intellectual belief regarding the immortal soul on a journey of evolution in one instant became a realization. Suddenly, I KNEW and faith came in. For without experience 'faith' is meaningless.

The second was the way it blew away the Ego. The illusion that 'I' was the doer was shattered and the meaning of surrender and humility before the divine seeped in. The fact that whatever comes to me in life is to teach me something was indeed humbling. It came to me because my soul needed it to learn a lesson and move on.

If poverty & suffering came it was to drive home a lesson but then so did wealth come .... to teach me something! And we, like fools tend to believe that wealth is always a reward... that we are special because we have gained success in life. Every individual tends to develop pride and arrogance under the illusion that he is the sole architect of his success. Even the success may have come at the cost of happiness, to teach us the value of happiness. It is not 'I' who has done something great. The 'I' has merely been sent something which would help it evolve – whether by appreciating what has been sent or realizing the futility of what has been sent for me to experience.

Interestingly, Agastya is not the only sage to have created such a work, there were others like Bhrigu also. But most of the other works have been scattered over a period of time and most are not in worthy hands. However, it does not take anything away from their merit.

'Naadi Jyotish', while showing me how I was bound by my 'Karma' also showed me how that very 'Karma' was also the way to freedom. It showed me that my past karma had laid out my destiny but I did have that degree of freedom to choose a path which would take me on to the destiny which awaited me on that alternate path. Each 'karma' of mine had a destiny inherent in it and the destiny would not allow me to skip any karmic lesson which was necessary for me as an evolving soul.

But the beauty is that, when I fulfill a 'karma' i.e., experience it with full awareness in its entirety, I am free from it. When I learn from an experience completely, life will not send it my way again. I shall be completely liberated from it. But until I do, it will remain a bondage.... a lesson due... and it will continue to haunt me... it will continue to come back.

The soul needs to learn & to evolve.... Agastya was not just telling my future in this birth, he was chronicling the journey of my soul as it unfolded over many births.......and thereby telling me something about my Being and its purpose.

> The fact that whatever comes to me in life is to teach me something was indeed humbling. It came to me because my soul needed it to learn a lesson and move on.

*"It is my feeling that Time ripens all things; with Time all things are revealed; Time is the father of truth." – Francois Rabelais*

## Nothing Really Goes Away

Sometimes when I drift back into the past it seems so full of events, images and people. Some bring a smile on my face, some a twinge of sadness but all of them are a part of me. Each and every memory still carries with it those emotions. My heart still flutters when I think of that beautiful girl; I still feel like crying at the death of my friend; I still feel the elation of my grand performance on stage; I still feel all the loving moments in my heart; I still relive the beauty of nature that touched me deeply,... all of these live on in my mind and heart.

The curious thing is, there is no sequence to all that went in and became a part of me. There is no order. There is no logic or sequence that governs all this. All the people and events in my life exist at the same time; always present – always coming back to hold me in their embrace. All these never really went away. Time in this context, seems an illusion. Nothing really goes away.

This middle aged happily married man is no different in essence from the twelve year old, who entered into a pact with his friend never to get married, nor is he any different from the infatuated and gawky teenager he once was. My drive, complexes, deep down desires & wishes all flow from the same source which hasn't changed one bit. Everything that has happened has only absorbed into me to become a part of me. All of it exists at the same time - within me. Everything that happened has always been there and will always remain within me. It is as if the love I felt, the despair I felt, the happiness I felt, the excitement I felt along with the people and the way I related to them are the deep realities and their placement in time and space has little meaning.

In the realm of feelings, which is the realm where we always remain - everything exists at the same time. All the people I love and relate with are there with me forever. Nothing really goes away.

All the people and events in my life exist at the same time; always present – always coming back to hold me in their embrace. All these never really went away. Time in this context, seems an illusion. Nothing really goes away.

*"From silence, the Universe crept up and whispered –'There is nothing that is not you'."*

# Where is God?

At this juncture of my life I can say with complete conviction: –

'As I am so the world is.'

I am convinced that there is no objective reality. You see the world in tune with your equipment of mind and body given to you. The 'objective reality' is nothing but the common perceptions and that too only to the extent they are shared by the creatures of the same species - in this case us human beings. Because we have the same biology we share the perception frozen by us from the quantum soup floating around. But when it comes to the mind - intellect combination coming into play the world starts becoming different for each one of us.

The 'objective reality' takes leave and we start squabbling - the communists with the capitalists, the Christians with the Mohammedans, the pessimists with the optimists and so on. Because the instruments of perception differ so does reality.

The perception ability available to you decides the world that you see, the gods that you believe in. The world of a dog or a bat is different from that of humans. Here is a commonality amongst humans because of the biological design of the human brain and sensory equipment available to you. This is what we fondly call 'objective reality' and take for granted. After this the reality perception also changes from person to person.

God is available to us in fragments. As we move up (evolve), more and more & bigger and bigger fragments appear before us.

As my awareness increases I am more alive to the world around me as if my consciousness perceives much more from the same old world and makes it available to me. Subtler levels of perceptions come into play, as if I had moved up a step and a far bigger picture lies before me. I become more rooted in subtler dimensions drawing my intentions and motivations from the realm of spirit - more rooted in love. The more I can grow, the more I can pierce the world around, whether it is matter or the human mind. This evolution also provides me with the God which I deserve, a more real and compassionate God. The God that is accessible to me, the god that I am entitled to, the God that I need for my further growth is the God that becomes available to me.

God therefore is a matter of deserving. My own state of being leads me to the extent of God which is meant to be revealed to me. Ultimately it must lead me to my becoming complete and perhaps discovering that I face myself. The world is as I am. What I am God is. The journey must bring me face to face with myself.

Because we have the same biology we share the perception frozen by us from the quantum soup floating around. But when it comes to the mind - intellect combination coming into play the world starts becoming different for each one of us.

*When it is dark enough, you can see the stars." – Ralph Waldo Emerson*

# Transformation

I stood on the raised platform in the Security area at the Airport as the security man frisked me. I was impressed with his thoroughness. There was nothing casual about it. He then took my purse and started rifling through the slot for coins. Suddenly it struck me that I had something in there which was dangerous... a .22 mm shell of a spent bullet which was given to me by A... more than 20 years ago and since he had expired a few years after that, the fragment of the bullet had remained with me. I always carried it in my purse as a memento of his remembrance.

Within seconds the security man held it up "What is this?" he asked. I was immediately removed to the back office. I knew I had made a big mistake by keeping that shell in my purse. But then it was something which had remained with me all this while. I had virtually forgotten about it and now it had landed me in a very big soup.

I was in deep trouble. While the security men were sympathetic there was nothing they could do for me. The law had to take its own course. The man in charge of the Security force was clearly in a dilemma. He knew I was innocent and yet he had to make an FIR and hand me over to the local police. The information had been transmitted to the highest officials of all the agencies concerned in seconds and within no time Delhi had been informed.

In spite of activating help at the highest of levels, I knew it was not going to be easy to get me out. The dear ones I called for help were trying frantically to get me out of the mess. Within a couple of hours I was handed over to the local police. The enormity of the situation was now ramming in very hard. The DSP was not willing to release me in spite of the FIR mentioning that I had been found to be innocent during interrogation.

I was sent outside the airport to a small cottage which served as the Police outpost. The security personnel who had registered the case came again for some formalities and the man who had searched me sat there with his eyes cast down. "Sorry" he managed to utter as he left. I shook hands and smiled reassuringly at him in a peculiar reversal of roles.

Then began the most despairing hours of my life....repeatedly I was told that nothing could be done for me. I could get bail only from a Magistrate, which might happen only the next day. More than likely I would be in custody for months as the precedence showed. In the wake of 9/11 these were very dangerous times. At the very thought, a shiver ran down my spine.

As dusk started to fall things were beginning to look very grim. Till now my mind was in a whirl. I had been praying desperately for help. I knew that the implications of the case could be very devastating if it stretched on. But I also felt completely powerless and helpless. There was nothing I could do, except stretch out for help in the mental realm. I was calling out to every God I had prayed to. Again and again I was calling out, seeking any kind of divine intervention. For I knew it would take an intervention of a divine nature to get me out. Nothing short of that was going to work.

It was the most critical point in my life. I was aware that one wrong turn here could ruin years of my life and reputation. In some ways the experience was devastating. As I look back I realize that internally I could have responded to the situation in different ways. I may have broken down completely and made an irreparable dent in my self respect. I could also have gone through the entire experience like a zombie – with little awareness.

But something entirely different happened. As I sat there looking out at the green foliage in the soft evening light I asked myself why I could not surrender when there was nothing I could do? Why couldn't I surrender to His Will? Out of the tremendous turmoil which was going on in my mind jumped out this feeling. Suddenly the frantic racing of the mind stopped.

It was as if I had stood aside and started looking at my self and my situation in a dispassionate manner. I had to admit that I did not have complete faith. I was not devout enough to leave myself in the hands of that Supreme Being. I had to accept that my intellect would not relent to faith.

And then as I sat I thought of my wife's love for me. I felt her palpable faith…. her unshakable and yet unreasonable belief that no harm would come to me. In my mind I could see her praying for me. More than anything else in those moments I truly and completely felt her love for me. And with that came peace. The turmoil inside me ceased. Amazingly I had no problem visualizing myself back with her. In that moment I knew I would be back with my family the next day.

I also understood that even though I may not be evolved enough to have complete faith, I was aware enough and sensitive enough to feel and respond to love. It was love that brought peace to me in those moments. From then on, I was completely calm and prepared to face whatever might come.

That moment of transformation showed me the power and value of love. That is what enabled me to surrender. In a way I felt Love was no different from faith. That was perhaps the divine intervention I was seeking. With surrender came a peace of the kind that I had never experienced before. In those moments of despair I had accessed an amazing reservoir of strength through the energy of love which had all along been there.

Within a few hours I saw the change in the physical realm. In the next hour the situation worsened and I was told so in so many words by the very persons on whom I was pinning my hopes. In spite of the best efforts at the highest levels, I was told no one was willing to stall or speed up the judicial process. Obviously they had not ceased trying but they were preparing me for the worst. It was the stage where I should have reached the depths of despair. But to my own surprise I remained unaffected. Yes, I knew it was grim and I was prepared to face whatever fate had to offer me. And yet, at another level I knew I would be home the next day.

And then suddenly & inexplicably, everything started moving in the right direction and by 8 p.m. I was free. In fact I was told to forget the whole thing as a bad dream. A nightmare it was indeed! But the paradox was that one of the most harrowing experiences of my life brought me face to face with the most beautiful thing in life.... the power of Love. I know that everyone who loved me prayed for me that day. But even beyond that was the man who tirelessly worked that day to get me released and he did it more out of his love for me than out of any sense of obligation or duty. And I know that this is a debt I can repay only through love.

For me now, Love has become something very tangible and concrete. Something through which we come face to face with ourselves – our own deeper reservoirs become accessible to us. To me love is now something through which divinity is accessible to us.....the very source of all strength and power, but which can be drawn only when you have the humility to surrender to it. I also know that this surrender may or may not reduce the challenges or the trials that may come my way but it will certain give me all the strength that I need to face them.

As I sat there looking out at the green foliage in the soft evening light I asked myself why I could not surrender when there was nothing I could do? Why couldn't I surrender to His Will? Out of the tremendous turmoil which was going on in my mind jumped out this feeling. Suddenly the frantic racing of the mind stopped.

*"Tell me and I'll forget. Show me, and I may not remember. Involve me, and. I'll understand." – American Indian Proverb*

# The Last Rites

There was a time I could not swallow some traditions of the Hindu Culture. A tradition which made the son, perform the last rites of his parents. How could people expect me to consign to flames the persons to whom I owed my very existence! How could you expect the son, to destroy with his own hands, the bodies of the people who brought him into this world! To me it always seemed a very cruel and heartless tradition.

Not till I had to perform the last rites of my mother could I begin to understand it.

But then the dreaded day came in my life as it had to. It was only then that I came to know that it was not merely a tradition – it was the ultimate entrustment of responsibility. It was also the only way I could have understood the difference between the person and the body left behind and yet have the same reverence for both. Having consigned my mother to the flames I also understood the deep bonding which was reinforced forever with that one last act. It must have been quite similar to the bonding she must have felt when she brought me into this world. Life had come a full circle. The eternal spirit must leave the most sacred of the responsibility – that of completing with dignity, the last rites of the vehicle it used in this life time – to his / her offspring.

Each and every act I performed that day was deeply seared into me. In that one act I became a parent from a son, the parent of my own parent. I carried the one who had carried me. She had taken care & responsibility of my frail and defenseless body as I was now taking care of hers. It was trust reposed in its most sacred form.

The eternal spirit must leave the most sacred of the responsibility – that of completing with dignity, the last rites of the vehicle it used in this life time – to his / her offspring.

*Significant achievements in life are never made except by people who are willing to forego opular approval in their quest for goals which their hearts tell them are right and true. –Omar Khayyam's Rubaiyat (Stanza seventy two)*

# Surviving Mediocrity

The society we live in seems to be very fond of mediocrity. If I have a secure job or income and I am in a rut - the people around me are happy. It does not matter if the individual in me is dying a slow and torturous death. It does not matter that this individual is doing things, which are far below him. He, according to the general standards earns a living, maintains a certain status, gets his quota of diseases by a certain age and dies a predictable death. Well, it is a decent enough life for a mediocre. But what if you don't consider yourself one? (*...and that is the real differentiator!*)

If you are not such a person - you cannot aim low. You may or may not succeed. But how many people appreciate the effort. People in general appreciate a rut. (*...success is to be admired from afar.. it is not for people like us!*) But should you really care?

I want to live life to the full. But one of the battles I have to constantly fight is the battle with people who are well meaning and concerned. People who want me to get into a secure rut. A rut, which may involve working for people who are inferior to me, people who would like to use me. But it is time now, for me to follow myself. As far as I am concerned, failing is not a crime – NOT TRYING is. I am not going to cave in to the lure of what is comfortable and easy.

The easy path has never appealed to me. I would like to take the path, less travelled. I would be insulting HIS gifts to me if I chose the life of comfortable mediocrity. I may end up with far less in terms of wealth. The standard of my living may be far less but my standard of life would be very high.

At least, at the end of the day I would be able to look into the eyes of the man whose opinion matters the most to me - the man who stares back at me from the mirror.

The standard of my living may be far less but my standard of life would be very high.

*He who made us must surely love us.*
*His reason for ordaining death*
*as the final act of life must, therefore, be*
*somehow connected with His Love. – Omar*
*Khayyam's Rubaiyat (Stanza sixty two)*

# Euthanasia

If the concept was not so disturbing I would be laughing. Death with dignity?...and what about the dignity of life itself? If euthanasia is justified, every suicide in the world is justified. The act of killing oneself and the law and society justifying it just because one is unable to bear the pain or just because the disease is terminal is a horrifying concept. One is giving in to the physical pain. Is that, reason enough to deny the purpose and beauty of life. One CAN face such a pain with dignity; it is a very flimsy ground to sanction the killing of someone. Is dignity accorded to death just because someone injects a lethal dose into you instead of your jumping in front of the speeding train?

Persons who commit suicide must be going through tremendous psychic or emotional pain - does it mean we should also approve of suicide! Why not, one might ask? After all such a person is going through much more than a terminally ill patient. He may be going through severe mental trauma; may have been socially ostracized; may have faced financial ruin; touched depths of self-esteem or gone through so many other torturous happenings. Legalizing suicide (as has been done in some countries) would be far more reasonable compared to euthanasia if one looks for reasons. And yet we have people lauding the legitimization of euthanasia in some countries.

Where does one really stop if the society starts off on a journey of such logic? Very soon you would have "reasons" enough to snuff out the life of the physically challenged or the mentally handicapped or the comatose. People would be arguing that such people do not "contribute" to society or do anything useful or that their condition cannot be improved. Family members of such people or some doctors with a few fancy degrees against their names would put a stamp of approval on such a decision. But are these criteria at all relevant when it comes to life. Life itself, cannot be judged by reason and logic alone. There would be no end to this insanity once we give in to such a heinous theory. Every moment of life has a purpose to it – the only problem is we do not have the required insight to understand it all the time. When we cannot even see the whole picture we have no right to decide when to end a human life.

Living a life of dignity till your last moment is what adorns your death with dignity. No one is wise enough to sanction or approve someone's death. Let us not play God for God's sake.

Since when has medical science become a predictive one? Death is beyond the prerogative of medical science. I wish doctors would not step into an arena, which is far beyond their competence. Their profession is noble because it demands reverence for life. Patients do revive after years of coma. Medical science recognizes the fact that healing is not the domain of medical science alone... that there are far more powerful forces of life like love, prayer and the will to live, working to keep a life going. One needs wisdom to understand such issues. Legitimizing euthanasia only indicates lack of spirituality. In the name of practicality we are always looking for shortcuts. A quick pilgrimage (but of course popular and happening one); a quick fix spiritual course; and now.... a quick fix death so that everything is over quickly. We want our own pain to end fast – the pain of having to bear the sight of someone we know suffer.

What a sense of relief one gets as soon as the last rites are over! But how difficult to keep doing what is required to be done when the suffering person is alive. How difficult to face the fact of oncoming death - How difficult to hold that person's hand –

how difficult to help ease the emotional pain – how difficult to speak meaningful words – how difficult to listen to his pain – how difficult to help him absorb the meaning of his own pain. It is so much easier to shut the door, isn't it!

In life, pain has as much meaning as happiness and pleasure. People who haven't experienced pain will never know the beauty of life. Whether you believe in soul or not, I cannot believe that the consciousness that I experience within me will end with this body. And if death is not the end of it all, every moment that is mine with this body has a purpose and meaning to it.

Yes, I do have the right to choose whether I shall resort to some kind of treatment or not. Whether I chose to hang on to some tried and tested unsuccessful methods of treatment or not. But certainly it is ironical if that very method which symbolizes failure in my treatment tells me that it has a poison to "end my suffering". But then refusing an aggressive treatment which is worse than the disease itself is quite different from euthanasia - which means actively killing a person and virtually requires a medical 'hangman'.

Isn't it better to leave the decision of when the end is to come to a higher consciousness which would know the right moment and the right means? A small part of the conditioned half of the human brain is not qualified to take this momentous decision.

God forbid, if I were to sanction the killing (brutal it may sound but that is what the fancy term Euthanasia means) of one of my loved ones, I do not think I could live with such a decision on my conscience. Human Conscience is the ultimate test of any decision. We can give any sophisticated argument to support any warped concept, but if it fails the test of our conscience... then every other argument is meaningless.

Whenever someone talks of Euthanasia I cannot help but think of 'Pundit' - the man who laughed through life, the man who was dignified in his simplicity. A pair of Kurta - Pyjama and a tremendous sense of humour was perhaps all he went around with. He remained a confirmed bachelor who found joy in every moment of living. And when he lay on his death-bed, his body emaciated due to the ravages of cancer - do you think he was asking for a lethal dose of injection? No. He was still making the people who came to him, laugh. He would still be cracking his one- liners like 'Death is a female that is why it is reluctant to come to me' Can someone say that he was not dignified in death! That man would grit his teeth if he had to but he would still give you his address in 'New Heaven, Love Circle' where he could be found after he left this world in a few days.

Pundit never let go of what he essentially was. Even through his searing pain he saw reasons to smile and make people laugh. He never despaired of life. He never lost the last of the human freedom

- the freedom of awareness, the freedom, which enabled him to see his own pain and yet make the choice of not suffering.

He knew that even his pain had a purpose. He chose a life of dignity. That is why death was humble when it approached him.

Sometimes I wonder what wisecrack he would have made if someone told him about euthanasia!

He never lost the last of the human freedom - the freedom of awareness, the freedom, which enabled him to see his own pain and yet make the choice of not suffering

*"Reality is merely an illusion, albeit a very persistent one." – Albert Einstein*

# The Possibility of Everything

I have always searched out astrologers, soothsayers, pundits – whoever had the ability to predict future events or provide solutions to life problems which apparently had no answers. Was I insecure? I never thought it that way. No one can really say that he is totally secure. For that matter no ordinary mortal can claim to have total faith in an Almighty power. So there is a natural urge in a person to try and know what the future holds in store for him. The fact that a lot of people choose to remain inactive in life and rely on soothsayers to bail them out is another problem altogether.

To me it was a search for a piece of truth. And a piece of truth is a piece of truth. It stands on its own. If people cannot handle it, it's their problem. Mankind has always had the talent of distorting such pieces of truth.

I was always drawn towards the mysterious. Always knew instinctively that there was much more to life than what was apparent. That is why again the occult sciences or arts (whatever one may wish to call them) held a fascination for me. Of course I did go through the rationalist phase in my life when I was convinced that everything under the sun could be explained by the logical part of the brain.

But slowly and surely I kept coming across instances and experiences which clearly showed that there one could have access to knowledge through some means and ways which had nothing to do with logic or reason. Whether it was a tattered horoscope predicting a divorce or another one predicting the year of death or a man in a trance warning about impending danger which looms up within hours or days – what fascinated me was not just that the future could be seen in some way, but more importantly, that the future already existed in some fuzzy dimension.

Not that everything that was predicted was accurate. But that was not relevant – precision was not the issue – the phenomenon was.

Again and again in life I was brought face to face with instances, which established to my mind that life functioned in its own mysterious ways. It would not follow a logical path to satisfy one-dimensional minds. Life would not conform to any pattern. A self-proclaimed rationalist at one point in my life, I was eating my words. Naturally people thought – 'What a turn-around'!

But it was not really a turn around. I had realized and added a richer and deeper dimension to my way of thinking. Logic and reason remained in their place – I had only discovered faculties and possibilities beyond mere reason and logic.

Who am I to deny the possibilities of this wonderful and mysterious universe? It is only the arrogance and vanity of man which makes him think that life should conform and fit into the mould he has created and should follow only the laws he has discovered. Ironically it is not the scientists who need this lesson rather it is a lesson to be taken by the people who keep talking of the age of science and believe that life restricts itself to the man made inventions that they have surrounded themselves with.

Reality winks at us from so many angles & ways and with so many intentions. That is the beauty. We live in a world where the possibility of everything exists. That is what makes life so exciting!

Whether it was a tattered horoscope predicting a divorce or another one predicting the year of death or a man in a trance warning about impending danger which looms up within hours or days – what fascinated me was not just that the future could be seen in some way, but more importantly, that the future already existed in some fuzzy dimension.

*"A foolish faith in a system has been the worst enemy of democracy."*

# The Stupid World Visions

This world has blamed science, technology, and modern weapons for destroying so much. But is there anything more poisonous than an ideology, which gives you its own world-vision and then gets people to kill for that utopia. It is never the weapon but the mind behind the finger that pulls the trigger that kills. It is the will to kill that kills. Therein lie the seeds of violence.

Time and again these diseases have been spread and humanity has paid a heavy price. Time and again we have been duped by such world visions. Sometimes these visions have been wrapped with religion, sometimes with social idealism.... but the common thing is that they have always sold a carefully crafted vision, which has been lapped up by hordes of people.

However, the fundamental truth that no ideology in the world is an answer to human problems seems to have escaped humanity. We need compassion and understanding as a basis for building societies.

We sit in living rooms and have intellectual discussions about how the 'wonderful' ideology could not be 'implemented' properly or wasn't 'understood'. Thus we go on sanctioning more such sick ideologies. Why don't we have the guts to denounce such ideologies per se – their philosophy – their fundamentals?

Humanity can chart its own course of evolution. We don't need iron-clad systems, utopias & world visions wherein 'believers' live happily ever after. Such ideologies deserve ridicule. Don't ban them. We only need to trash them.

Time and again we have been duped by such world visions. Sometimes these visions have been wrapped with religion, sometimes with social idealism.... but the common thing is that they have always sold a carefully crafted vision, which has been lapped up by hordes of people.

*"Much that passes as idealism is disguised hatred or disguised love of power."*
*–Bertrand Russell*

# The Man in the Rubber Slippers

It was the fag end of seventies. The Naxalite* movement had been crushed in West Bengal. I was studying to become a Chartered Accountant and as part of the course working as an articled clerk then. With a senior I was sent to Singur in the suburbs of West Bengal to conduct the audit of a Cold Storage. It was more of a village than a town. The cold storage was the only notable thing about the place. The only source of entertainment we had was a small black and white TV in the Manager's mini cottage.

Since the assignment would last more than a month and food would be a problem, we hired a cook. Unfortunately my colleague was a hard man to please and within a fortnight the cook we had taken with us was fed up with the behaviour of my senior and walked out in a huff one fine day. Now, we had no choice but to hire a local man. Soon enough this lanky man in thick glasses and rubber slippers turned up. It was obvious that cooking wasn't his profession. But as long as he could cook up a decent meal, it was fine with me.

We again settled into a routine, until the time my colleague again threw a tantrum one day and insisted on yogurt. Our cook who was in the middle of his work was quite reluctant to go and do the errand but my colleague was adamant. The cook was wild but ultimately did go and do the job. Red faced with anger and muttering in English he banged the packet of curd on the makeshift dining table. Not only was he a man with a lot of pride, he was quite obviously educated. I was curious. It turned out he held a post graduate degree in Arts.... an MA and a cook? I was disturbed. Slowly his story came out. By the time he had finished his studies he was deeply into the Naxalite movement. He had been caught by the police and brutally tortured. He received the worst part of the beating on his feet. Apparently he was tied up and repeatedly hit on the soles of his feet with batons. The beating was so severe and prolonged that the nerves in his feet were badly damaged. Since then he could not wear anything but rubber slippers on his feet.

The man cooked for us till the end of our stay. As soon as our audit was over we packed our bags and said our good byes. In fact I was glad that the monotonous job was over. The platform was quite empty and I settled down on a bench to wait for the local train. Suddenly I looked up to see our friend, the cook, standing there with his bicycle. He had come to see us off. I could see he was very emotional. I patted him on his shoulder when I saw tears welling up in his eyes. Such display of emotions for someone he had only known for a fortnight? I was really taken aback. Here, was another dimension to this man, I was surprised again. There wasn't much I could say.

The train was there in a few minutes. We got on and I saw that he was still where I had left him standing on the platform. He stood there, unmoving – tears rolling down his cheeks, the bicycle leaning against his thin frame. As the train rolled out I looked back one last time at the man in rubber slippers. I left the place with a feeling of sadness.... at a brutalized and wasted life. Wasted for the sake of an ideology, which like so many other ideologies, was nothing more than a disease – an ideology which led sensitive men like him astray.

And all that it left behind as a legacy was the pain of dealing with life in a pair of rubber slippers.

**[This was a movement which started off against the exploitation of farmers but then degenerated into mindless killings to create a new order. It was an ultra* *left movement wherein a number of political leaders, landlords, merchants and even traffic constables were killed in public places to send a message across. The movement has since spread to other parts of India]*

I left the place with a feeling of sadness….at a brutalized and wasted life. Wasted for the sake of an ideology, which like so many other ideologies, was nothing more than a disease – an ideology which led sensitive men like him astray.

*"What you are screams so loudly in my ears, that I cannot hear what you say!" – Emerson*

# Living at the Core

Change is one thing all of us are so used to seeing all around us. Throughout our lives we see people, circumstances and places changing. Change is indeed the only constant factor we perceive. At the same time we attribute these changes to so many things. All the time we seem to be pushed to the logical conclusion that there are factors, which seem to be shaping us....which determine as to what we are going to become.

We see people change radically once they come into money or become famous or fall into bad days. People seem to change when they get power; they seem to change when they get fame. So we have learnt to assign the responsibility of our being to the genetic, social, environmental factors and so on.

Over the years I also perceived changes within myself and around me. Of course the changes within, seemed so much more tangible. I did not need any convincing that I was changing or that

I had changed. Through all the travails, events, shocks, grief & joyous moments I found myself, changing steadily. In a way I was responding to whatever was happening in my life and happening TO me as a direct consequence. In terms of learning, social standing, wealth, position I have traveled. And yet…in my heart of hearts I was not convinced that I had indeed changed. Why did this feeling persist?

I still feel that I have been shaped by the boy I was. The boy who used to save the drowning ants in his bathroom still has a say, in my life. I know I would still do that. So have I really changed? What I have deeply believed in has only become firmer over the years. So am I right in thinking that I have changed. Yes, at times, I did forget some of the principles and values that were a part of my inherent psyche. But nevertheless, they were always there and they did prevail. The basic characteristics of my persona did not change.

The paradox is very real. I think most of us are aware of it in some way or the other. At one level we seem to be changing all the time and at another nothing really ever changes.

Obviously change requires a closer look. Or rather what changes requires a closer look. I suppose we exist at the core as much as we exist at the circumference. Although both are a part of my being they are in a way different from one another (another paradox!) The periphery keeps responding to the environment, but the core is not so easily affected by things and events. We tend to judge people by what we see at the circumference. And when we see them respond or react to circumstances, we conclude that they have changed. But then we have never really seen their core. It is only exceptional circumstance or the small things in life, which reveal the true face of a man. The typical day to day living hides so many flaws for it does not demand anything out of a person. The masks are so much firmly in place.

The gracious socialite can be seen at her obnoxious best when she deals with her servant. The suave businessman's true face can be seen when he dupes his own friends in the name of business. The meanness or the large hearted-ness of a friend is revealed through small and apparently small actions. The apparently jovial woman at the picnic shows her true colors when she cuts the largest piece of cake for her own child. The apparently trivial things can tell us a lot about a person. The qualities of a man appear as soon as he is thrown into a life-threatening situation; the large-hearted man shares even in adversity. One can never judge a man by how much he spends. You judge him by his ability to give even though it pinches him. He does not give because he can afford it, he gives because it is his nature to give. It simply shows the level of his evolution. True character always shows we must learn to see it.

Gold is always gold, no matter where you put it. In life we need to appreciate the intrinsic worth of people and not their positional worth. In the

Bagatelle of life, our positional worth changes with every swing.

A particular ball which lands in the high number slot in one round may land up as zero in yet another round. And sometimes it ends up at 'L.T.P.' or 'Lost Total Points'. Put me where you will, it cannot change what I am! I may say or have apparently different behaviour at different points of time, but that is only at the periphery. What needs to be seen is whether the essential characteristics have changed.

As birthday gifts, my friend N, always gave me, what he considered to be the most valuable gift of all.... a new book. He gave me this gift even at a time he could ill afford it, at a time when every rupee mattered to him. Even at the time when he was struggling to survive. He still gifts me with this thing that he considers most precious. His personal fortunes have undergone an appreciable change – he hasn't. The size of heart does not change with the size of the purse.

WHAT I am has never really changed! But yes HOW I am at the moment does keep changing from moment to moment. Deep down inside me, at the very core I remain what I am. There are things, which affect this core, but those things have to be very profound to have an impact. And certainly THINGS do not have the power to bring about that change. Only values and feelings can. Tremendous prosperity or adversity tear off the carefully applied masks and reveal the true character of a person.

They do not change the person… they only reveal him. We manage to see him for what he is.

The apparent lifestyle, the manner of dealings, the social standing of a person may change. But that is no criteria of judgment. That change is limited to the circumference. Look for the core, it always reveals itself.

What we are, is not determined by the stimulus from the external world. But our response to the stimulus does reveal what we are. Financial and social status does not make us, but how we respond to this change shows what we are made of.

People are fond of quoting a very old saying – "Money is the root of all evil." But the truth is that this saying is misunderstood and misinterpreted like our reading of people. The actual saying goes – "The love of money is the root of all evil." If we can understand this difference, nothing else remains to be explained.

Tremendous prosperity or adversity tear off the carefully applied masks and reveal the true character of a person. They do not change the person… they only reveal him. We manage to see him for what he is.

*"Reality leaves a lot to the imagination."*
*– John Lennon*

# Give your Attention to Make it Real

All that has been created by human being first appeared in his mind before it took shape in the physical world. And the one factor, which was responsible for making it appear as a human creation was his belief. Only the thoughts, which were backed by belief or given sufficient mental energy, made it to the physical realm. Why only the physical realm.... for that matter, all that we give our mind to, is real for us.

"Believe in it and it is nothing less than a God... don't and it is a mere stone!" Thus goes a very old saying. A saying I never understood till recently. I had never seen the power of the mind. The ever increasing, number of Gods in the Hindu society continued to fox and amaze me. No matter how much I read I found no answer anywhere.

Then I saw the palpable belief of the people towards the thousands of Gods they worshipped. With every fiber in their body they believed in the power of their deity. And wonder of wonders it worked for them. Slowly, I had encounters where these deities communicated with the people. In spite of all the question marks that still remain. I was convinced beyond doubt that one way or the other whoever or whatever these deities might be. The more mind energy they were given the stronger and more effective they were. They were as much real as the temples that housed the idols were. Reality it seems to me is inextricably entwined with what we believe in. At least in part it is a function of our belief. Our mind energy is instrumental in creating that reality; otherwise how does one explain faith healing, which cuts across all religions and globe.

The fact that medical science cannot explain it does not take away an iota out of this reality.

All this seems far-fetched when one talks in the above terms. But consider the facts thrown up by quantum physics – the fact that there is no such thing as physical matter. Matter is only a ripple in space. Any phenomenon in the universe is inextricably linked to the observer. There is no happening in the universe, which is not affected by the perceiver.

To me, quantum physics seems more far fetched than the belief of a common man. But the simple finding that does emerge is that the mind is not only the window to reality, it seems to be the canvas of reality. Since we are merely scratching the surface of the individual mind, the glimpse of the collective mind on which this universe has been sketched seems to be as remote as the farthest galaxy streaking away from us.

Nevertheless, we seem to be able to create our realities. That is a power gifted to us.....a power which is inherent in us. The simplest path would be to believe in all that is good. Because all that we give our mind to, is destined to be real. In that sense we are the masters of our destiny. When we see it in our minds, we see it in our lives.

Whatever I gave my mind to, did come to pass in life. And whenever I failed to do so it did not. The failure was only on that count. The mind did not fail. It was I, who failed to put it in the right direction and focus its intensity. Every time I succeeded in putting my mind to it, the magic did unfold. Life opens up wherever our attention is focused.

Life opens up wherever our attention is focused.

*Live behind the scenes of relative time,*
*in the unchanging present.*
*Only by living properly right now,*
*at the changeless center of the moment,*
*can we arrive at that point, where we exercise*
*complete control over our lives.*
*–Omar Khayyam's Rubaiyat*

# Lessons from a Tomato Eater

The train sped away into the darkness. And in our dimly lit coach, he sat there on the side berth - a man of considerable bulk. He sat there staring into the darkness - not really looking at anything for there was nothing to see. But the reason my attention went to him was the fact that he sat there with a tomato in his hand - a raw tomato. And then I saw him take it to his mouth and bite into it, his eyes now half closed. There was that serene look on his face as if he was in meditation. He bit into the tomato as if it was the most natural thing on earth to do. Not a drop of the juice was spilt on his shirt or anywhere else for that matter.

My attention was riveted on him. He was enjoying the tomato with all his being. This is what I was identifying with, not the tomato or its effects. He seemed to be totally absorbed in the process of eating and I was totally absorbed by what he was absorbed in. It was as if the tomato itself wanted to willingly disappear into him. I could see the oneness and harmony in that simple act of eating the tomato. That day I understood the meaning of living life fully. I also understood the meaning of present moment living. That moment and that act are significant in my mind because it was a profound lesson wrapped in a simple act. It taught me that there is always something to savour. It taught me that 'right now' can be a wonderful moment in life as long as I allow it to be so- as long as I make it so.

There is always a tomato around. All we have to learn is to how to really eat it.

That moment and that act are significant in my mind because it was a profound lesson wrapped in a simple act. It taught me that there is always something to savour. It taught me that 'right now' can be a wonderful moment in life as long as I allow it to be so- as long as I make it so.

*"Love and doubt have never been on speaking terms."*
*– Khalil Gibran*

# The Destroyer

Whenever there has been a doubt, whatever I have wanted has not happened. Doubt has destroyed.

At every point in life, one wants something – one expects something. I suppose it is human nature. The mind always conjures up something – an achievement, a success, a relationship, a piece of happiness or a sweet touch. We are always ready to receive, in fact eager to receive and yet most of the time what we want does not crystallize.

What our mind creates, it also destroys. In fact we destroy it ourselves. It takes a lot of positive mental energy to build something but only the seed of doubt to devastate the most beautiful of our dreams.

When we doubt, we do not see, we do not believe. And what we do not believe; can never come true. Whenever there is doubt there can be no dream –

no vision. When we doubt, dreams die, only fantasy remains.

Doubt is the negation of the thought at its very origin. So the thought never really manifests itself in this physical world. Doubt creates conflict and disharmony within. And where there is conflict and disharmony there can be no creation – no manifestation. But have you noticed the play of the divine? Doubt also comes when you know you are wrong. It may come when the heart is not pure. It comes when we do not deserve what faces us. It also comes when we are weak. It comes when we wish to possess. It never comes when we simply want to express; it does come when we wish to impress. It never comes when we wish to achieve but it does come when we want success.

Doubt exists about expectations, never really about what we essentially are. We all know our own character, so we also know the temptations we may succumb to.

We face the real challenges of doubt when we set out with our aims. That is the time when doubt emerges as the destroyer. Our doubts are not about what we are; they are about what we can do.

But when we have the courage of conviction, when we are on the side of good, doubt rarely stays with us. When there is good will doubt does not touch us. When we are rooted in convictions, it leaves our very being.

When our intentions are right, may we never doubt – for doubt is death!

Doubt is the negation of the thought at its very origin. So the thought never really manifests itself in this physical world. Doubt creates conflict and disharmony within. And where there is conflict and disharmony there can be no creation – no manifestation.

But have you noticed the play of the divine? Doubt also comes when you know you are wrong. It may come when the heart is not pure. It comes when we do not deserve what faces us. It also comes when we are weak. It comes when we wish to possess. It never comes when we simply want to express; it does come when we wish to impress. It never comes when we wish to achieve but it does come when we want success.

*"Only two things are infinite, the universe and human stupidity, and I'm not sure about the former."*
*–Albert Einstein*

# Science Alone is not the Answer

We have reached a time of glib answers, a time, when the very ability to wonder, has lost out to vague assumptions – a time, when the arrogance of people is matched only by their ignorance. The irony is that people swear by the science which itself has learnt humility in the last few decades.

We live in a time when a whole lot of fundamental questions about life & living seem to have lost their deeper significance for most people. Most of us seem to believe that what science has not discovered does not exist. The wisdom of the information age seems to suggest that, what science cannot explain does not really require an explanation. We seem to have mortgaged our thinking to the establishment of science, but the irony is that scientific approach has lost its relevance.

The deepest of mysteries of nature are dismissed by the silliest of comparisons or smug answers. So 'the brain is nothing but a computer'; 'life is just a state of matter'; 'organs like tonsils and appendix do not have any function to play' and 'rational mode is the highest mode of thinking'; 'intuitive knowledge cannot be termed knowledge'.... and so on....

For a long time, organised religion took on the mantle of dealing with such issues. Today we are convinced, that the establishment of religion has failed mankind in so many ways – that the only answer lies with science!

Millions believe that perhaps it is science, which would provide the answers. People have been convinced now for centuries that science would pierce this veil of mystery. But are we getting any closer? We have got a whole lot of newer mysteries brought to light, but no light on any of the mystery itself. The veil remains firmly in place.

The simple fact is that mysteries are to be lived and understood and not unraveled. Any process of thinking which sets out to analyze a mystery is already doomed. For you can only decipher a process not the phenomena itself. The living frog can be dissected to see how it lives – but no amount of poking the organs can answer WHY it lives!

The science of light and its behavior can perhaps describe in detail, what happens during that colourful sunset. But it cannot explain even an iota of the joy and beauty my heart feels when I watch it.

The mystery of the sunset is answered just by experiencing it completely. Laughter is what is to be enjoyed, how we laugh has little relevance!

No doubt science has its uses and is necessary for our physical survival. But why do we expect to fulfill a role it was never equipped to handle? The highest of science today is pointing towards the mystery and beauty of existence – not answering and unraveling or analyzing it.

It is time to understand that science is not really the answer, it is only a means of raising new questions – pointing out newer mysteries. Therein, lies its beauty and utility!

The answers to life lie in living through the miracle of life. Science or the rational mode of thought is only one note in the rhythmic harmony of the song of life.

The science of light and its behavior can perhaps describe in detail, what happens during that colourful sunset. But it cannot explain even an iota of the joy and beauty my heart feels when I watch it.

*"Wisdom has its root in goodness, not goodness its root in wisdom."– Ralph Waldo Emerson*

# The Saint with a Cover Drive

We live in a cynical age. An age where charlatans abound; where leaders have feet of clay; where religion is an industry; where doctors operate only for money; where business is an excuse for cheating; where godmen amass wealth by deceit..... an age where nothing seems genuine, nothing seems good, nothing seems pure and nothing provides solace to the weary heart of the common man who seems doomed to live a life between despair & despair.

It seems almost as if we have been abandoned by God. It seems as if he no longer cares enough to send saints, seers & sufis amongst us. Saints who would show us the right way to live… a way which would keep us happy... a way which would put us in touch with ourselves…

But then we are wrong! When have we ever recognized a saint while he walked amongst us?

This time also we failed to recognize him. He entertained us for 24 years. He gave us hope, he gave us pride, he gave us honour.... he gave us a reason to look forward to a better tomorrow. When he played India forgot to breath. He became a part of our lives. When he played we became Indians... we became One!!

Indian Cricket was never the same once he walked onto the scene. They say he always seemed to have a lot of time to play his shots. But what was seldom realized was that only a man in a meditative state could have that kind of time to play his shots. There were times he zoned out and it was only between him and the ball hurling towards him at 150 km/hour. All this went beyond being just a skilled player. This was the 'here & now' saint – one who was always in the present moment and knew just how to handle it.

But people saw him only as a Cricketer albeit a great one. He has millions of fans who were mesmerized with the way he played. However, the people who played with him came to know him as a great friend, guide, competitor and a wonderful human being. But some of them really saw beyond that. They saw a man who had been touched. And who in turn could touch and transform people around him.

His life was all about a single minded focus on the passion of his life. It was a lesson in how to achieve. Success was completely incidental to that achievement. Day in and day out he only lived to perfect his art. He was never focused on the result. And then he went on to show how to meet success without losing all that is human in us.

He lived what was preached in the Bhagwad Gita. His life was not just to be seen – his life was worth emulating. His life could tell you what was going wrong with yours. His life could tell you how to live yours. His life made you believe that you only had to give your 100% and the rewards would come. When you saw him you knew what equanimity was.... neither praise nor criticism disturbed his poise.

No sledging, no abuse, no rancour, no bragging, no negativity through 24 years of intense International level competition.... he could fight without being anyone's enemy – because he was devoid of any malice. He did not talk about spirituality, he showed us what spirituality is... a life devoid of ego. He showed how one could be unaffected by all the accolades and riches in the world. He lived all the philosophies, advice and the pathways shown in the scriptures. If you clearly saw his life you did not need a commandment to follow.

Sachin Ramesh Tendulkar is a modern saint.... he just came in a different garb. He sported India-colours instead of saffron and carried a willow instead of a kamandal. He did not preach, he simply lived the way a modern day saint should. He is the saint of these times and therefore his message came through a life we could identify with. Millions lived their dreams through him.

He had a message for every one. The day he retired, he made me ask myself – "Have I given my 100%?" I had never described myself as a typical

Sachin fan. I had never been one of those who said Sachin is God! But the day he retired I felt something profound had gone out of my life. The way he thanked the people in his life made millions cry. I wept because I was touched … I wept because his gratitude ignited similar feelings in me. He also made me question my own life. How can I have a life as fulfilling as the one I witnessed and which was only half way through?

'Bolne ka nahin...karne ka hai' is not just what he said... it is the way this saint has lived. With every milestone, he just looked up towards the heavens in gratitude. He acknowledged the divine working through him. He made himself an ego-less instrument.... and that is why the divine shone through him... that is what made him a saint.

But you know what? I don't want to touch your feet Sachin... I just want your soul to touch mine!!

Day in and day out he only lived to perfect his art. He was never focused on the result. And then he went on to show how to meet success without losing all that is human in us.

*"Most people say that it is the intellect which makes a great scientist.*
*They are wrong: it is character."*
*– Albert Einstein*

# Where do we go Wrong?

I do not believe there is anyone who does not possess a unique gift – a gift that he came into this world with; a gift or talent that makes him so different from the others – a gift that defines him – a talent that sets him apart.

We come into this world uniquely individual, with our own secret mission, which we need to discover. In discovering that mission, lies the unraveling of the purpose of our own unique journey. In this understanding lies our fulfillment.

Yet the irony is that most of us never really discover our own unique talent. Most of us never really get around to finding what makes us tick. We never really get around to discovering, what in essence we actually are.

Our time in this world is spent in wanting, consuming and competing – never really in discovering. In the whole process of growing up, education and then the pursuit of a livelihood we never really have time for self-discovery. The whole education designed to fill us up with all the knowledge in the world does not devote itself to the process of self-discovery.

This world has lost millions of prodigies, because they never discovered their own uniqueness. Wonderful cooks spent their lives building bridges, talented singers spent their lives teaching mathematics & brilliant surgeons lived through the drudgery of tending to counters of their family business. And humanity lost out on a more harmonious and peaceful world.

Is it not time to ask ourselves – 'Where do we go wrong?'

I do not believe there is anyone who does not possess a unique gift – a gift that he came into this world with; a gift or talent that makes him so different from the others – a gift that defines him – a talent that sets him apart.

*"May you have enough happiness to make you sweet, enough trials to make you strong, enough sorrow to keep you human and enough hope to make you happy."*

# The Profound is Trivial and the Trivial is Profound

In existence everything is complete with a paradox. Man has conditioned himself into believing that whatever he considers important enjoys a similar divine sanction as well. But the reality does not conform to his ego.

The story of our lives is a story of one long struggle, a struggle to reach lofty objectives…a long social climb… a life dedicated to a social cause…a life spent chasing a mirage…an unending attempt to whet our appetite for wealth…a chase for job satisfaction… a life of with only the destination in mind. But at the end of the day our lives have been a long story of missed moments.... of a journey completed without any awareness of the beauty missed by the wayside.

We have conditioned ourselves into believing that chasing utopias is a profound objective. Not realizing that the trivial piles up into something far greater than the so called profound.

Too late do we realize that a smile on the face of our child is what lent meaning to our lives...it was the time spent with your ailing mother that was precious... it is the walk through the public park with your wife when you did not have that car that is still fresh in your mind...your fondest memory is that of your son winning that race and not the JV that you signed.

Too late we realize that life was always made up of the so called trivial.....the so called profound was just a space-filler. The profound was up there but the trivial was right there in our heart.

All the utopian ideals, lofty dreams, ambitions, social causes, environmental concerns, political dreams were profound aims & objectives. Yet at the end of each day we always longed for the embrace of the loved one, the smile of an offspring, the hug from a friend, the gratitude of the deprived, the sheer joy displayed by your pet when he saw you, the sight of plants after a monsoon shower, a dip in the sea, your terrace washed by the moonlight, the feel of the warm sun on a winter morning, the touch of your mother's hand on your feverish brow, the pat on your back from your father....all that was trivial but all that made life meaningful.

We never really achieve the profound but we always live and cherish the trivial.

Sometimes I do wonder what is trivial! And what really IS profound?

But at the end of the day our lives have been a long story of missed moments.... of a journey completed without any awareness of the beauty missed by the wayside.

# Epilogue

Every life is so very unique. This uniqueness has a purpose. A purpose we are meant to discover. Whatever happens to us is designed to help us discover that very purpose. Every life, every incident, every relationship appears... to teach us something. Directly or indirectly, every person that we meet is telling us something.

At the behavioral level we react to situations and people. But at a much deeper level our soul responds to each person in a unique fashion. It is this interaction that we try to decipher so that we may decipher ourselves. And even beyond that, unless we delve into our lives deep enough and take time to examine it we can never understand our own intrinsic nature.

When all is done & dusted – what matters is how much we evolved and how much, did we help others to evolve. Did I touch lives? Did I make a difference where it mattered? Could I reach deep down inside a person and touch his soul? If I could not, all my achievements count for little!

No matter how much we argue about science & rationality, deep down within ourselves, we know that we are not an accident produced by molecules. In the ultimate analysis, in our own way, all that we are doing is to try and understand this human life that we have been endowed with.

When you listen to the call of your soul you stop & contemplate on your life... it is only then that you go on to understand it... and it is only then that you can make it worth living!!!

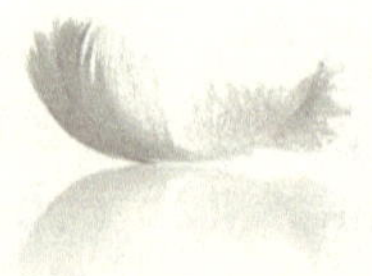

www.ingramcontent.com/pod-product-compliance
Lightning Source LLC
LaVergne TN
LVHW042343150826
845671LV00001B/3

* 9 7 9 8 8 9 4 7 5 7 3 4 6 *